Digital Drawing for Designers

A Visual Guide to AutoCAD

DIGITAL DRAWING FOR DESIGNERS

A Visual Guide to AutoCAD

Douglas R. Seidler

New England School of Art & Design

at Suffolk University

Fairchild Publications, Inc.

New York

Director of Sales and Acquisitions: Dana Meltzer-Berkowitz

Executive Editor: Olga T. Kontzias

Acquisitions Editor: Joe Miranda

Senior Development Editor: Jennifer Crane

Development Editor: Michelle Levy

Art Director: Adam B. Bohannon

Production Manager: Ginger Hillman

Senior Production Editor: Elizabeth Marotta

Copyeditor: Chris Reeves

Cover Design: Adam B. Bohannon

Cover Art: Douglas R. Seidler

Text Design: Ron Reeves

Library of Congress Catalog Card Number: 2006933711

ISBN: 978-156367-512-6

GST R

Certain images and materials contained in this text were reproduced
with permission of Autodesk, Inc. © 2006. All rights reserved.

Printed in Canada

TP 14

CONTENTS

EXTENDED CONTENTS

PREFACE

Objective

This book provides designers a visual, clear, and concise guide to better understand the world of digital drawing as it relates to AutoCAD. While there are many AutoCAD books on the market, most are thick with technical language and excessive technical discussions about the software. In my experience, many discussions in these books use inconsistent language or complicated instruction to teach relatively simple tasks. These books also require the learner to choose which information is essential to understand AutoCAD, something that poses a great challenge to many students. After teaching digital drawing at Suffolk University for several years, I recognized that architects and interior designers need better AutoCAD instruction.

Recent educational research suggests that students gain a stronger understanding through instruction with specific and transparent learning objectives. In addition, the research suggests that understanding is easier to attain when learning connects to a body of knowledge that the student already understands. For AutoCAD, the existing body of knowledge seemed obvious: manual drafting.

The combination of my in-class teaching experience and this educational research inspired me to develop and write supplemental course material that better communicates the relationship between AutoCAD and manual drafting. Through this new approach to teaching AutoCAD, I found that my students' enthusiasm and general understanding of AutoCAD increased exponentially. This supplemental course material became the foundation for this book. I wrote *Digital Drawing for Designers* to share this new teaching approach with architects and interior designers in colleges and universities across the country.

Audience and Prerequisite Knowledge

AutoCAD continues to dominate the two-dimensional drafting marketplace for architects and interior designers. This book aims to help the design community by visually teaching for understanding. You can broadly sort the numerous AutoCAD books into two categories—"guides for dummies" and "exhaustive references"—neither of which specifically addresses how professional designers use AutoCAD. *Digital Drawing for Designers* sits between these two categories, providing both a thorough primer for new learners and expanded conceptual discussion for design professionals. The progressive introduction of concepts (chapters build on previous chapters), printed exercises, and visual examples make this book easy to follow for learners new to AutoCAD. Learners with little or no understanding of AutoCAD should look through Chapters 1 and 2 to see how easy it is to visually learn AutoCAD.

While I developed the material in this book for the university classroom, it also seems appropriate as an office reference for both junior and senior design professionals. Since each page within the book is designed to maximize learning, professionals can quickly access or re-learn specific AutoCAD concepts and commands. Senior designers, required to transition to digital drawing, will understand the lessons in this book more readily than traditional AutoCAD manuals due to the pedagogical connection back to manual drafting. Learners with a basic understanding of AutoCAD should look through Chapter 11 to see the depth of discussion for setting up and adding dimensions to your drawings.

The only prerequisite for the book is a fundamental knowledge of manual drafting techniques.

AutoCAD Version Compatibility
The instruction in this book is compatible with AutoCAD version 14 through version 2007. Most universities teach and use the latest version of AutoCAD. Most professional offices do not annually update their AutoCAD software due to hardware requirements and professional education costs. I have written this book to help students switch between versions of AutoCAD as they transition from the classroom to the office. I anticipate that this book will be compatible with future releases of AutoCAD software.

Content Overview
We learn best when we can create connections between the new information we are learning and information that we already know. Chapters 1–4, therefore, introduce AutoCAD and digital drawing through the language and concepts of manual or hand drawing. Lines, circles, and arcs are the fundamental building blocks of all architectural drawings. Understanding how to use these building blocks in AutoCAD will allow you to create any type of drawing.

Chapters 5–8 introduce you to graphic standards that will help you use AutoCAD to create drawings that communicate your design ideas. Understanding these standards keeps you in control of your drawing and allows you to "ask of the computer" rather than let the computer dictate how your drawings will look. You will also learn organizational strategies to efficiently draw plans, sections, and elevations. Each chapter introduces these new skills using AutoCAD standards that can be adapted to any office environment.

The final four chapters introduce many advanced AutoCAD concepts like dimensioning drawings, creating your own drawing stencils, and linking drawings. Learners that have a basic understanding of AutoCAD will appreciate the in-depth visual discussion about Xrefs, editable blocks, dimension styles, and text leaders. By combining these advanced concepts with a strong foundation for drawing in AutoCAD, you will be prepared to work on or create any digital drawing.

We all know the promise that mastering AutoCAD will save you time and energy. By following the step-by-step guides in this book you will master digital drawing in AutoCAD by building your confidence and understanding of the software. In addition, it is my hope that through the visual guides and pedagogical approach of this book you will become a better designer by strengthening your understanding of how to communicate your designs through digital drawing.

—DOUGLAS R. SEIDLER

ACKNOWLEDGMENTS

This book began several years ago as a reader for a series of design drawing and AutoCAD courses offered by the Department of Interior Design at the New England School of Art and Design at Suffolk University. The strategies for teaching and learning used in this book are largely influenced by my experience teaching AutoCAD and by *Teaching for Understanding*, a course for design educators taught by Tina Blythe at the Boston Architectural College.

I would like to thank the students and instructors whose discussions, critical feedback, and enthusiasm helped shape and test the pedagogical approach of the material in this book. Special thanks are due to Cheri Kotsiopoulos, Kristine Mortensen, and Lori Anderson Wier for contributing their drawings to this book.

I also greatly appreciate the enthusiasm, guidance, and collaboration of the team at Fairchild Books. The efforts and talents of Olga Kontzias, Jennifer Crane, Michelle Levy, Liz Marotta, and Adam Bohannon are more than I could have asked for in an editorial team.

Finally, I would like to extend my appreciation to my parents, my sister, and my wife Patricia for their continued support and enthusiasm over the last year.

Digital Drawing for Designers
A Visual Guide to AutoCAD

HAND DRAWING AND DIGITAL DRAWING

CHAPTER 1
Digital Drawing Tools

This chapter introduces you to AutoCAD's digital drawing techniques and tools using a visual vocabulary that you are already familiar with from your experience with manual drafting. One of the best ways to learn something new is to refer to something you already know.

By the end of this chapter, you will be familiar with the AutoCAD equivalents to many of the drawing tools you use daily in manual drafting.

Drafting Table
· Used to hold your paper during the drawing process. AutoCAD is the digital equivalent of your drafting table.

Pencil
· Used to draw a line. The AutoCAD equivalent is the **LINE** command.
· See page 12 to learn about drawing lines.

Parallel Bar, Triangle, T Square
· Used to draw horizontal and vertical lines. The AutoCAD equivalent is **ORTHO**.
· See page 14 to learn about drawing with Ortho.

Eraser
· Used to erase lines that are no longer needed or were drawn in error. The AutoCAD equivalent is the **ERASE** command.
· See page 13 to learn about erasing lines.

Eraser Shield

· Used to erase lines to a specific point. The AutoCAD equivalent is the **TRIM** command.
· See page 40 to learn about trimming lines.

Architectural Scale/Ruler

· Used to draw lines at a specific distance or length. The AutoCAD equivalent is the **UNITS** command.
· See page 22 to learn about setting units.

Compass

· Used to draw circles. The AutoCAD equivalent is the **CIRCLE** command.
· See page 16 to learn about drawing circles.

Protractor

· Used to draw lines at an angle. One AutoCAD equivalent is the **ROTATE** command, which allows you to rotate lines at an angle.
· See page 30 to learn about rotating lines.

AutoCAD (Drafting Table)

The window below represents the typical AutoCAD interface.

· Many of AutoCAD's menus and buttons are similar to those of other programs (e.g., Microsoft Word, Excel, and PowerPoint).
· This book introduces AutoCAD's gizmos, buttons, and menus as it introduces drawing concepts and techniques.
· You can use the index at the back of this book to quickly find additional information about a particular AutoCAD command or concept.

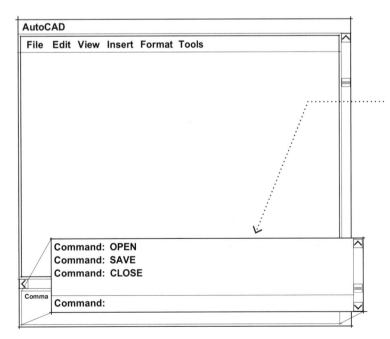

AutoCAD

File   Edit   View   Insert   Format   Tools

New
Open
Close

Save
Save As
Export

Page Setup Manager
Plot
Plot Preview

Command:

Menu Bar

· You may be familiar with many of the drop-down items on the menu bar if you have used a program like Microsoft Word.
· Items under the **FILE** menu allow you to **OPEN**, **CLOSE**, and **SAVE** your AutoCAD drawings.

AutoCAD

File   Edit   View   Insert   Format   Tools

Command: OPEN
Command: SAVE
Command: CLOSE

Comma

Command:

Command Prompt

· Most commands in AutoCAD are started by typing on the keyboard in the command prompt.
· The command prompt area in AutoCAD also provides feedback about options during a command.
· Keep one eye on the command prompt as you work and you will improve your AutoCAD learning experience.

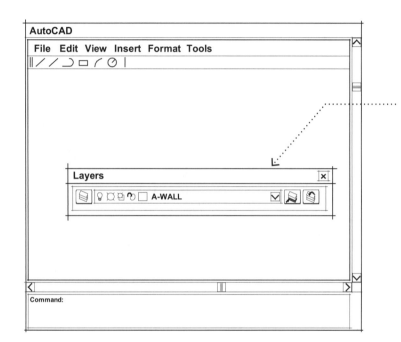

Button Bar

· In addition to the command prompt, most commands in AutoCAD can also be started with a button. Because buttons change their appearance and location from one version of AutoCAD to the next, this book encourages you to use the keyboard commands rather than the buttons when drawing in AutoCAD.

· Using the keyboard and command prompt to start commands (in lieu of buttons) provides a more efficient way to draft.

· Close floating button bars by clicking the **X** in the upper right corner.

Tool Palettes

· Newer versions of AutoCAD contain tool palettes that allow you to start some commands.

· Using the keyboard and command prompt to start commands (in lieu of tool palettes) provides a more efficient way to draft.

· Close the tool palettes by clicking the **X** in the upper right corner.

Pan

- When you draw in AutoCAD, your drawings are limited by the size of the screen. The **PAN** command allows you to slide your drawing around on the screen in the same way you could slide a piece of paper around your drafting table.

- The **PAN** command slides your drawing around on the screen without changing the size of the drawing on the screen.
- Type the command **PAN** and press **ENTER**.
- Your mouse cursor will change to a **HAND**. With the mouse, **CLICK AND DRAG** in your drawing. You will notice that the drawing follows your cursor around the screen.
- Press the **ENTER** or **ESCAPE** key to end the Pan command.

Pan with the Mouse

- You can also start the **PAN** command with the scroll wheel on your mouse. The scroll wheel is also a mouse button. With the mouse scroll wheel, **CLICK AND DRAG** in your drawing. You will notice that the drawing follows your cursor around the screen.
- The **PAN** command automatically ends when you release the scroll wheel button.

Zoom

· When you draw in AutoCAD, your drawings are limited by the size of the screen. The **ZOOM** command allows you to move closer to and farther away from elements in your drawing.

Zoom Window

· Zoom window allows you to enlarge a specific part of your drawing by drawing a window around it.

· Type the command **ZOOM** and press **ENTER**.
· **Step 1**: The zoom command asks you for the first corner of the zoom window. Drag the AutoCAD cursor to the top left of the area you want to enlarge and **CLICK ONCE**.
· **Step 2**: The zoom command asks you for the second corner of the zoom window. Drag the AutoCAD cursor to the location on the screen where you want the lower right corner of the area you want to enlarge and **CLICK ONCE**.

Zoom Extents

· Enlarges or shrinks your drawing to fit entirely on the screen.

· Type the command **ZOOM** and press **ENTER**.
· Type the command **EXTENTS** and press **ENTER**.

Zoom with the Mouse

· Use the scroll wheel on your mouse to enlarge or shrink your drawing dynamically.

· The scroll wheel on your mouse is also a button. If you **DOUBLE CLICK** on the scroll wheel, AutoCAD will perform the **ZOOM EXTENTS** command.

Guide for Success

I encourage new AutoCAD users to practice drawing as soon as possible. Consider the following challenges to help you through this book.

· Draw the examples/projects provided at the end of each chapter.
· Draw a room in your home.
· Draw a design project you have already drawn by hand.

Companion Downloads

The following web site features companion downloads for each chapter in this book:

http://www.fairchildbooks.com/book.cms?bookId=179

· Download learning exercises to practice different drawing tools covered in this book.
· Download from over 20 sheet templates to start almost any type of drawing.
· Download sample plans, elevations, and sections to see how professionals draw using AutoCAD.

CHAPTER 2
Drawing Lines and Shapes

Lines, circles, and arcs are the fundamental building blocks of all design drawings. By the end of this chapter you will have a strong understanding of the means and methods to draw these elements in AutoCAD.

Consider the following questions as you work through this chapter:

· What are the relationships between fundamental manual drawing skills and their AutoCAD command equivalents?
· How are drawing units configured in an AutoCAD drawing?
· What is drawing precision, and what tools help you achieve it in an AutoCAD drawing?

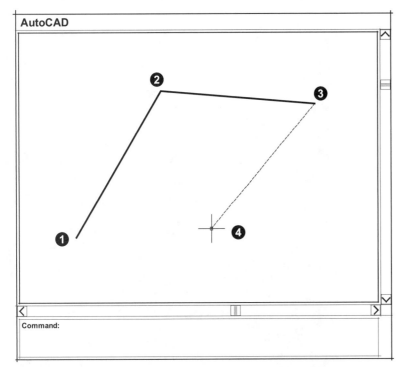

Line (Pencil)

In AutoCAD, you use the **LINE** command to draw straight lines. The manual drafting equivalent to the **LINE** command is drawing a line with a pencil and a straight edge.

Drawing Your First Lines in AutoCAD

- Open AutoCAD on your computer.
- Using the keyboard, type the command **LINE** and press **ENTER**.
- **Step 1**: Using the mouse, **CLICK ONCE** in the lower left of the AutoCAD drawing area. As you move the drawing cursor around the screen, notice how AutoCAD shows you a straight line.
- **Step 2**: **CLICK ONCE** in the drawing area of AutoCAD following the diagram on the left.
- **Step 3**: **CLICK ONCE** in the drawing area of AutoCAD following the diagram on the left.
- **Step 4**: Press **ENTER** on the keyboard to end the **LINE** command.

Erase (Eraser)

In AutoCAD, you use the **ERASE** command to erase lines that are no longer needed or were drawn in error.

Erasing Lines in Your Drawing

· Type the command **ERASE** and press enter. In the command prompt (at the bottom of AutoCAD), the erase command prompts you to select the objects you want to erase. For now, we will cover the easier methods to select objects in AutoCAD.

· **Method 1**: To erase all the lines in your drawing, type the command **ALL** and press **ENTER**. Press **ENTER** to complete the erase command.

· **Method 2**: To erase selected lines in your drawing, **CLICK ONCE** on the lines you want to erase, one at a time. When you are finished selecting lines to erase, press **ENTER**.

· **Method 3**: Draw a **WINDOW SELECTION** around the items you want to erase. Every line or object that is completely within this window will be selected (and erased).

· To draw a **WINDOW SELECTION, CLICK ONCE** on the left side of the objects you want to erase. As you drag the mouse to the right, you will see a window on the screen. **CLICK ONCE** on the second corner of the window. When you are finished selecting lines to erase, press **ENTER**.

· **Method 4**: Draw a **CROSSING SELECTION** that touches the items you want to erase. Every line or object that this crossing selection touches will be added to the selection (and erased).

· **CLICK ONCE** on the right side of the objects you want to erase. As you drag the mouse to the left, you will see a window on the screen. **CLICK ONCE** on the second corner of the window. When you are finished selecting lines to erase, press **ENTER**.

Ortho (Parallel Bar, T Square)

In AutoCAD, you use Ortho to draw horizontal and vertical lines much the same as you use a parallel bar or T square on a drafting table to draw horizontal and vertical lines.

F8

Drawing Horizontal and Vertical Lines

· The F8 button on the keyboard toggles the Ortho Mode between on and off.

· Clicking the Ortho button at the bottom of the AutoCAD screen will also turn the Ortho Mode on and off.

Command:

| SNAP | GRID | ORTHO | POLAR | OSNAP | DYN | LWT | MODEL |

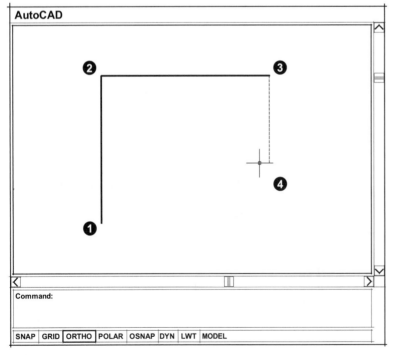

AutoCAD

Command:

| SNAP | GRID | ORTHO | POLAR | OSNAP | DYN | LWT | MODEL |

· Using the keyboard, type the command **LINE** and press **ENTER**.
· **Step 1a**: Using the mouse, **CLICK ONCE** in the lower left of the AutoCAD drawing area.
  As you move the drawing cursor around the screen, notice how AutoCAD shows you a straight line.
· **Step 1b**: Press **F8** on the keyboard.
  As you move the drawing cursor around the screen, notice how AutoCAD now shows you only horizontal and vertical lines.
· **Step 2**: **CLICK ONCE** in the drawing area of AutoCAD following the diagram on the left.
· **Step 3**: **CLICK ONCE** in the drawing area of AutoCAD following the diagram on the left.
· **Step 4**: Press **ENTER** on the keyboard to end the **LINE** command.

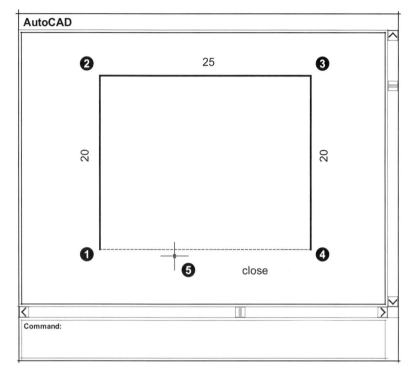

Drawing Lines at a Specific Distance

- Using the keyboard, type the command **LINE** and press **ENTER**.
- **Step 1**: **CLICK ONCE** in the lower left of the AutoCAD drawing area. Press **F8** on the keyboard to turn Ortho Mode on.
- **Step 2**: Drag the AutoCAD cursor upward on the screen. Type **20** on the keyboard and press **ENTER**.
- **Step 3**: Drag the AutoCAD cursor to the right on the screen. Type **25** on the keyboard and press **ENTER**.
- **Step 4**: Drag the AutoCAD cursor downward on the screen. Type **20** on the keyboard and press **ENTER**.
- **Step 5**: Type **CLOSE** on the keyboard and press **ENTER**.

- The Close command draws a line from the last point entered to the first point. (In our drawing, the Close command created a line from Step 4 to Step 1.)

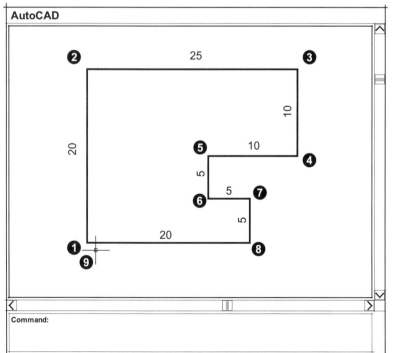

Drawing Exercise

- Practice drawing lines at specific distances by redrawing the sketch to the left.

- Erase everything in your drawing before you begin this drawing.

Drawing Circles

In AutoCAD, you use the **CIRCLE** command to draw a circle. The manual drafting equivalent to the **CIRCLE** command is drawing a circle with a compass. We will look at the three most common methods to draw a circle in AutoCAD.

Circle	Two-Point Circle	Three-Point Circle
Unless you specify otherwise, Auto-CAD will draw a circle the same way you draw a circle with a compass. You will need to know the center of the circle and the length of the radius.	When you draw a two-point circle, you are actually drawing a line that represents the diameter of the circle.	When you draw a three-point circle, you are actually defining three points that are on the edge of the circle. This method is used infrequently.

  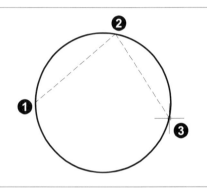

- Type the command **CIRCLE** and press **ENTER**.
- **Step 1**: CLICK ONCE in the drawing area where you want the center of your circle.
- **Step 2**: Drag the AutoCAD cursor in any direction on the screen. Type **15** on the keyboard and press **ENTER**. In this example, **15** is the radius of the circle.

- Type the command **CIRCLE** and press **ENTER**.
- Type the command **2P** and press **ENTER**. (This is your way to tell AutoCAD you want to draw a two-point circle.)
- **Step 1**: CLICK ONCE in the drawing area where you want the left edge of your circle.
- **Step 2**: Drag the AutoCAD cursor in the right direction on the screen. Type **30** on the keyboard and press **ENTER**. In this example, **30** is the diameter of the circle.

- Type the command **CIRCLE** and press **ENTER**.
- Type the command **3P** and press **ENTER**. (This is your way to tell AutoCAD you want to draw a three-point circle.)
- **Step 1**: CLICK ONCE in the drawing area where you want the first edge of your circle.
- **Step 2**: Move the AutoCAD cursor in any direction on the screen and **CLICK ONCE** in the drawing area where you want the second edge of your circle. (You will not see anything on the screen until you mouse click the second point of the circle.)
- **Step 3**: Drag the AutoCAD cursor in any direction on the screen and **CLICK ONCE** in the drawing area where you want the third edge of your circle.

Drawing Rectangles and Polygons

You can increase your drafting speed by allowing AutoCAD to help you create specific kinds of shapes like **RECTANGLES** and **POLYGONS**. You can use the rectangle and polygon command to create equilateral triangles, squares, pentagons, and hexagons.

Rectangle

AutoCAD will draw a rectangle or square when you provide the location of two opposite corners. (You are drawing the diagonal of the rectangle.)

Inscribed Polygon

An inscribed polygon can have three or more sides and will fit inside a specified circle.

Circumscribed Polygon

A circumscribed polygon can have three or more sides and will fit outside a specified circle.

  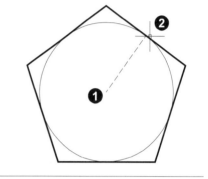

- Type the command **RECTANGLE** and press **ENTER**.
- **Step 1: CLICK ONCE** in the drawing area where you want the lower left corner of your rectangle.
- **Step 2:** Drag the AutoCAD cursor up and to the right. **CLICK ONCE** in the drawing area where you want the upper right corner of your rectangle.

Alternate for Specific Sized Rectangles

- Type the command **RECTANGLE** and press **ENTER**.
- **Step 1: CLICK ONCE** in the drawing area where you want the lower left corner of your rectangle.
- **Step 2:** On the keyboard, type **@10",30"** and press **ENTER**. AutoCAD will draw a rectangle that is **10** inches wide and **30** inches tall. (Of course, you can change the 10 and the 30 for rectangles of other sizes.)

- Type the command **POLYGON** and press **ENTER**.
- AutoCAD will ask you how many sides you want for your polygon. Type the command **5** and press **ENTER**.
- **Step 1: CLICK ONCE** in the drawing area where you want the center of your polygon.
  AutoCAD will ask you if you want to create an inscribed or circumscribed polygon. Type the letter **I** (for inscribed) and press **ENTER**.
- **Step 2:** Drag the AutoCAD cursor to the right on the screen. Type **30** on the keyboard and press **ENTER**.

- You have created a five-sided polygon that sits inside a circle with a radius of 30 inches.

- Type the command **POLYGON** and press **ENTER**.
- AutoCAD will ask you how many sides you want for your polygon. Type the command **5** and press **ENTER**.
- **Step 1: CLICK ONCE** in the drawing area where you want the center of your polygon.
  AutoCAD will ask you if you want to create an inscribed or circumscribed polygon. Type the letter **C** (for circumscribed) and press **ENTER**.
- **Step 2:** Drag the AutoCAD cursor to the right on the screen. Type **30** on the keyboard and press **ENTER**.

- You have created a five-sided polygon that sits outside a circle with a radius of 30 inches.

Drawing Arcs

The **ARC** command allows us to draw part of a circle. The manual drafting equivalent to the **ARC** command is drawing a circle, semicircle, or arc with a compass. We will look at the three most common methods to draw an **ARC** in AutoCAD.

Arc – Three Points

Unless you specify otherwise, AutoCAD will draw an arc based on three points along the arc.

Arc – Center, Start, End

Using the Center option, AutoCAD will draw an arc the same way you draw with a compass. You will need to know the center of the arc, the start point, and the end point.

Arc – Start, Center, End

This is a variation on the previous method of drawing an arc. You will need to know the start of the arc, the center point, and end point.

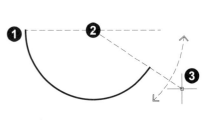

- Type the command **ARC** and press **ENTER**.
- **Step 1:** CLICK ONCE in the drawing area where you want the first point of your arc.
- **Step 2:** Drag the AutoCAD cursor in any direction on the screen. **CLICK ONCE** in the drawing area where you want the second point of your arc.
- **Step 2:** Drag the AutoCAD cursor in any direction on the screen. **CLICK ONCE** in the drawing area where you want the third (end) point of your arc.

- Type the command **ARC** and press **ENTER**.
- Type the letter **C** (for center) and press **ENTER**. (This is your way to tell AutoCAD you want to draw an arc by its center.)
- **Step 1:** CLICK ONCE in the drawing area where you want the center of your arc.
- **Step 2:** CLICK ONCE in the drawing area where you want the start of your arc.
- **Step 3:** CLICK ONCE in the drawing area where you want the end of your arc.

- Type the command **ARC** and press **ENTER**.
- **Step 1:** CLICK ONCE in the drawing area where you want the start of your arc.
- Type the letter **C** (for center) and press **ENTER**.
- **Step 2:** CLICK ONCE in the drawing area where you want the center of your arc.
- **Step 3:** CLICK ONCE in the drawing area where you want the end of your arc.

Drawing Ellipses

An ellipse looks like a stretched circle. AutoCAD creates the shape of an ellipse by two axes that define its length and width. The longer axis is called the major axis, and the shorter axis is called the minor axis.

Ellipse – Two Axes

Unless you specify otherwise, Auto-CAD will draw an ellipse based on the length of the two axes.

Ellipse – Center, Axis, Axis

AutoCAD can draw an ellipse based on the center point and the length of the two axes.

Ellipse – Angled

AutoCAD can draw an ellipse tilted on an angle. The angle of an ellipse is set by the first axis you draw.

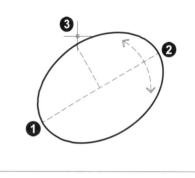

- Type the command **ELLIPSE** and press **ENTER**.
- **Step 1**: **CLICK ONCE** in the drawing area where you want the start of your first axis.
- **Step 2**: Drag the AutoCAD cursor in any direction on the screen. **CLICK ONCE** in the drawing area where you want the end of your first axis.
- **Step 3**: Drag the AutoCAD cursor in any direction on the screen. **CLICK ONCE** in the drawing area where you want the end of your second axis.

- You can specify distances in the **ELLIPSE** command the same way you specify distances in other commands, like line and circle.

- Type the command **ELLIPSE** and press **ENTER**.
- Type the letter **C** (for center) and press **ENTER**. (This is your way to tell AutoCAD you want to draw an ellipse by its center.)
- **Step 1**: **CLICK ONCE** in the drawing area where you want the center of your ellipse.
- **Step 2**: Drag the AutoCAD cursor in any direction on the screen. **CLICK ONCE** in the drawing area where you want the end of your first axis.
- **Step 3**: Drag the AutoCAD cursor in any direction on the screen. **CLICK ONCE** in the drawing area where you want the end of your second axis.

- Type the command **ELLIPSE** and press **ENTER**.
- **Step 1**: **CLICK ONCE** in the drawing area where you want the start of your first axis.
- **Step 2**: Drag the AutoCAD cursor in any direction on the screen. **CLICK ONCE** in the drawing area where you want the end and angle of your first axis.
- **Step 3**: Drag the AutoCAD cursor in any direction on the screen. **CLICK ONCE** in the drawing area where you want the end of your second axis.

- The axes in an ellipse are always perpendicular to each other.

- You can also use the Rotate command to change the angle of an ellipse you have already drawn.

Object Snaps

In a good AutoCAD drawing, lines connect to each other at precise points (the end of a line, middle of a line, or intersection of two lines). Object snaps allow you to start or end lines at a precise point relative to something you have already drawn.

Using Object Snaps

Object snaps can be activated during most AutoCAD commands. While you are in a command, hold down the **SHIFT** key and **RIGHT CLICK** to activate the Object Snap menu. Select the desired object snap and continue with your command.

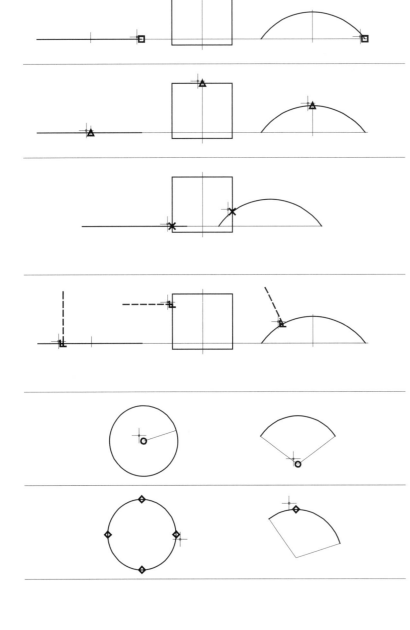

· Endpoint – Snaps to the endpoint of a line, circle, or arc. Also snaps to the closest corner of a square, rectangle, or polygon. Endpoint can be used as the first or second point when drawing a line.

· Midpoint – Snaps to the midpoint of a line or arc. Also snaps to the midpoint of any side of a square, rectangle, or polygon. Midpoint can be used as the first or second point when drawing a line.

· Intersection – Snaps to the intersection between any two of the following: line, arc, circle, square, rectangle, or polygon. Intersection can be used as the first or second point when drawing a line.

· Perpendicular – Snaps to create a new line that is perpendicular to a line, arc, circle, square, rectangle, or polygon. Perpendicular is mostly used as the second point when drawing a line.

· Center – Snaps to the center of an arc or circle. Center can be used as the first or second point when drawing a line.

· Quadrant – Snaps to one of the four quadrants of an arc or circle. Quadrant can be used as the first or second point when drawing a line.

Running Object Snaps

Object snaps can be set to activate automatically as you draw in Auto-CAD. (You do not need to use the shift right-click method described on the previous page).

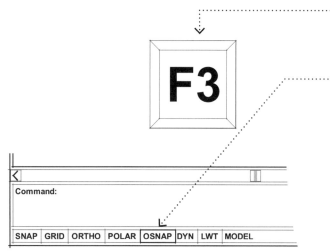

- Pressing the **F3** button on the keyboard toggles the Running Object Snap mode between on and off.

- Clicking the Snap button at the bottom of the AutoCAD screen will also turn the Running Object Snap mode on and off.

Setting the Running Object Snaps

When you use running object snaps, it is important to be specific about which object snap modes you want turned on.

- Type the command **OSNAP** and press **ENTER**.
- **UNCHECK** the Object Snap Tracking On option.
- Check on the following modes: **ENDPOINT, MIDPOINT, CENTER,** and **INTERSECTION**.
- **CLICK OK**.
- These four running object snaps will increase your accuracy and productivity for almost everything you draw in AutoCAD.
- Use the **SHIFT RIGHT-CLICK** method if you need to activate a different object snap.

- It is recommended that you do not draw with the perpendicular or nearest running object snaps turned on. These two object snaps (in Running Object Snap mode) are responsible for 90 percent of all drawing inaccuracies.

Drawing Precision

There are many things to consider when evaluating the craft of a manually drafted drawing. For example, you must keep your lead or pencil sharp, maintain a clear and legible line weight, and draw line length with precision. Similarly, the extra time you spend now to master these skills in AutoCAD will help you tremendously when you start your first drawing.

Setting the Drawing Units

Most likely, you will want to draw in AutoCAD using feet and inches or the metric system. AutoCAD allows you to draw using either unit of measure.

· We will use feet and inches as the primary drawing units in this book.

· To set the drawing units in AutoCAD, type **UNITS** and press **ENTER**.

Drawing Units [x]

- Length
  Type:
  Architectural ▽
  Precision
  0'-0 1/32" ▽
- Angle
  Type:
  Decimal Degrees ▽
  Precision
  0 ▽
- Insetion scale
  Units to scale insert
  Inches ▽

OK   Canc

Drawing Units [x]

- Length
  Type:
  Decimal ▽
  Precision
  0.00 ▽
- Angle
  Type:
  Decimal Degrees ▽
  Precision
  0 ▽
- Insetion scale
  Units to scale inserted content:
  Inches ▽

OK   Cancel

· **Feet and Inches** – Set the Length Type to **ARCHITECTURAL** and the Length Precision to **1/32"**.

· **Metric** – Set the Length Type to **DECIMAL** and the Length Precision to **0.00**.

Using Feet and Inches

In a good AutoCAD drawing, lines are drawn at precise lengths (i.e., 1'-6"). If you are precise when drawing lines in AutoCAD, you will find huge benefits at later stages in your project.

· Pressing the **SPACE BAR** in AutoCAD is the same as pressing **ENTER**. Use the hyphen (-) instead of pressing the space bar when entering units.

Methods to enter 2' 6"

· type **30"** and press enter
· type **2.5'** and press enter
· type **2'6"** and press enter
· type **2'-6"** and press enter

Methods to enter 2' 6½"

· type **30.5"** and press enter
· type **2'6-1/2"** and press enter

Using the Undo Command

The **UNDO** command allows you to step backward in your drawing and undo the last command. For example, if you erased a line that you did not want to erase, the Undo command would put that line back in your drawing. AutoCAD will undo all the way back to the point when you opened your drawing.

Undo Quickly

· The quickest way to use the Undo command is to press the **CTRL** key and the letter **Z** at the same time (**CTRL+Z**). This will undo the most recent command.
· You can use **CTRL+Z** multiple times to undo a series of commands.
· The shortcut for the Redo command is **CTRL+Y**. This will redo your last undo.

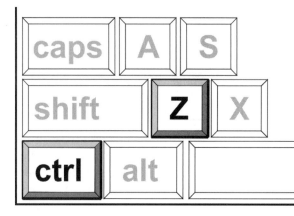

Undo Multiple Steps

The Undo command also allows you to undo several steps at once. This is helpful if you know that you want to undo the last five commands.

· Type the command **UNDO** and press **ENTER**.

· AutoCAD will prompt you for the number of commands you want to undo. Type **5** and press **ENTER**. AutoCAD will undo the last five commands.

· If you want to undo back to the point when you opened your drawing, ask AutoCAD to undo an extremely large number of commands (e.g., 10,000).

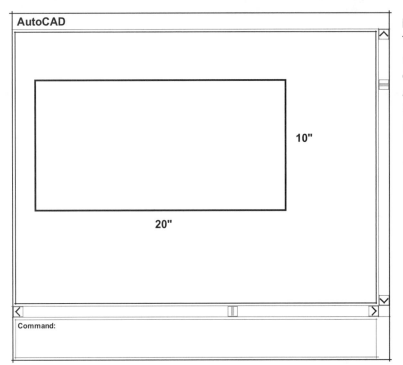

Learning Exercise

The following exercise will help you better understand drawing shapes and lines using object snaps. There are additional exercises available for download at http://www.fairchildbooks.com/book.cms?bookId=179

·   Draw a **RECTANGLE 20"** wide by **10"** high.

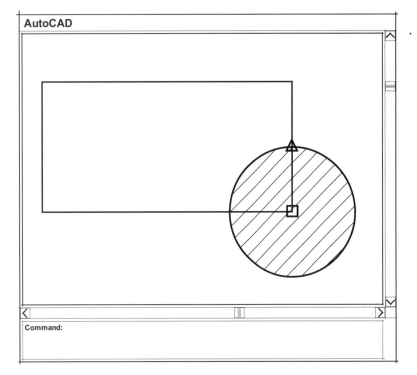

·   Draw a **CIRCLE** from the lower right **ENDPOINT** of the rectangle. The radius of the circle is the **MIDPOINT** of the rectangle.

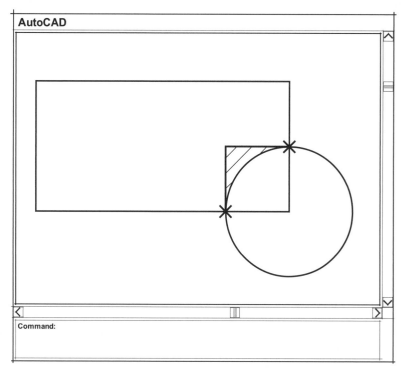

AutoCAD

Command:

· Draw two lines that start at the **INTERSECTION** of the circle and the rectangle.

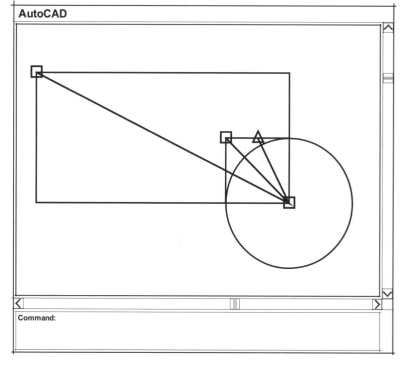

AutoCAD

Command:

· Draw three lines using the **ENDPOINT** and **MID-POINT** object snaps.

CHAPTER 3
Modifying Lines and Shapes

If you have ever typed a letter on a typewriter, you understand how word processing software like Microsoft Word saves you time and energy during the editing process. This chapter introduces many of the editing commands in AutoCAD. These concepts and commands will help you more efficiently edit your design drawings.

Consider the following questions as you work through this chapter:

· What are the different editing tools in AutoCAD, and how do they relate to their manual drawing equivalents?
· How much longer does it take you to draw in AutoCAD versus drawing by hand?
· How much longer does it take you to edit your drawings in AutoCAD versus editing your hand drawings?

Move

There is no efficient manual equivalent to the **MOVE** command in AutoCAD. If you need to move lines on a manually drafted drawing, you must erase the lines and re-draw them in their new location. The **MOVE** command allows you to literally pick the lines up off the paper and place them in a new location on the paper.

Moving Lines in Your Drawing

- Type the command **MOVE** and press enter.
- The Move command asks you to select the objects you want to move. You can select objects to move using the exact same selection methods we discussed with the Erase command in Chapter 2.
- Select the lines in your drawing that you would like to move (we selected the entire rectangle in the example to the left). When you are finished selecting lines to move, press **ENTER**.
- **Step 1:** The Move command asks you for the base point of your move. **ENDPOINT** snap (shift + right click) to the lower right corner of the rectangle.
- **Step 2:** The Move command asks you for the second point of your move. Drag the AutoCAD cursor to the location on the screen where you want the lower right corner of the rectangle and **CLICK ONCE**.

Move a Specific Distance

- Type the command **MOVE** and press **ENTER**.
- Select the lines in your drawing that you would like to move and press **ENTER**.
- **Step 1:** Click anywhere on the screen. Turn Ortho on by pressing the **F8** key.
- **Step 2:** Drag the AutoCAD cursor in the right direction on the screen. Type **20"** on the keyboard and press **ENTER**.

Move a Distance Over and Up

- Type the command **MOVE** and press **ENTER**.
- Select the lines in your drawing that you would like to move and press **ENTER**.
- **Step 1:** Click anywhere on the screen. Turn Ortho on by pressing the **F8** key.
- **Step 2:** Drag the AutoCAD cursor to the right on the screen. Type **@20",10"** on the keyboard and press **ENTER**.
- The horizontal distance is 20" and the vertical distance is 10".

Copy

There is no efficient manual equivalent to the **COPY** command in AutoCAD. Many designers use trace (translucent paper) to re-draw lines and then move the trace around as an overlay to their original drawing. The **COPY** command allows you to literally pick the lines up off the paper and copy them in a new location on the paper. We use the **COPY** command the same way we use the **MOVE** command.

Copying Lines in Your Drawing

- Type the command **COPY** and press **ENTER**.
- The copy command asks you to select the objects you want to copy. Selection methods are discussed with the erase command in Chapter 2.
- Select the lines in your drawing that you would like to copy (we selected the entire rectangle in the example to the left). When you are finished selecting lines to copy, press **ENTER**.
- **Step 1:** The Copy command asks you for the base point of your copy. **ENDPOINT** snap to the lower right corner of the rectangle.
- **Step 2:** The Copy command asks you for the second point of your copy. Drag the AutoCAD cursor to the location on the screen where you want the lower right corner of the new rectangle and **CLICK**.
- Press **ENTER** to end the Copy command.

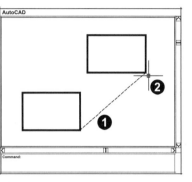

Copy a Specific Distance

- Type the command **COPY** and press **ENTER**.
- Select the lines in your drawing that you would like to move and press **ENTER**.
- **Step 1:** Click anywhere on the screen. Turn Ortho on by pressing the **F8** key.
- **Step 2:** Drag the AutoCAD cursor in the right direction on the screen. Type **20"** on the keyboard and press **ENTER**.
- Press **ENTER** to end the Copy command.

Copy a Distance Over and Up

- Type the command **COPY** and press **ENTER**.
- Select the lines in your drawing that you would like to move and press **ENTER**.
- **Step 1:** Click anywhere on the screen. Turn Ortho on by pressing the **F8** key.
- **Step 2:** Drag the AutoCAD cursor in the right direction on the screen. Type **@20",10"** on the keyboard and press **ENTER**.
- Press **ENTER** to end the Copy command.

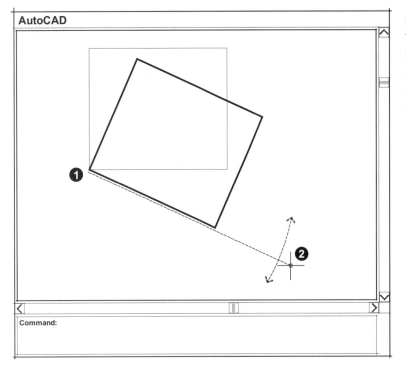

AutoCAD

Command:

Rotating Lines in Your Drawing

There is no efficient manual equivalent to the **ROTATE** command in AutoCAD. The **ROTATE** command allows you to rotate lines around a pivot point and place them in a new location on the paper.

· Type the command **ROTATE** and press **ENTER**.
· The rotate command asks you to select the objects you want to copy. Select the lines in your drawing that you would like to rotate (we selected the entire rectangle in the example to the left). When you are finished selecting lines to rotate, press **ENTER**.
· **Step 1**: The Rotate command asks you for the base point of your rotate (this is really the pivot point of your rotation). **ENDPOINT** snap to the lower left corner of the rectangle.
· **Step 2**: The Rotate command asks you to specify the rotation angle. Drag the AutoCAD cursor to the right and up and down to see your rectangle dynamically rotate. **CLICK ONCE** when you find the desired angle.

AutoCAD

Command:

Rotating Lines at a Specific Angle

The rotation shown in the example above is not very precise. We can precisely rotate a line or lines at a specific angle.

· Type the command **ROTATE** and press **ENTER**.
· Select the lines in your drawing that you would like to rotate and press **ENTER**.
· **Step 1**: The Rotate command asks you for the base point of your rotation. **ENDPOINT** snap to the lower left corner of the rectangle.
· **Step 2**: The Rotate command asks you to specify the rotation angle. Type **-30** on the keyboard and press **ENTER**.

· Positive angles (e.g., **30**) in AutoCAD rotate objects counterclockwise.

· Negative angles (e.g., **-30**) in AutoCAD rotate objects clockwise.

MIRROR (REFLECT) LINES

Mirroring/Reflecting Lines in Your Drawing

The **MIRROR** command allows you to make a mirror image of (or flip) a line or group of lines in your drawing. This is the same concept as taking a drawing on translucent paper and folding the paper along a line. The lines you see through the back of the paper are the mirror image.

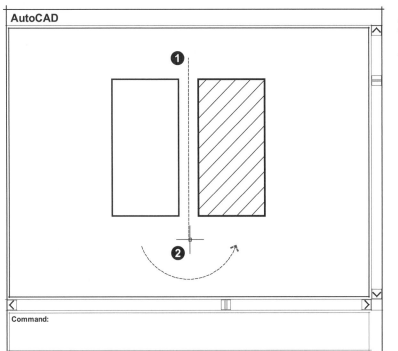

Mirroring Lines in Your Drawing

The **MIRROR** command requires that you draw an imaginary mirror line to reflect your lines.

- Type the command **MIRROR** and press **ENTER**.
- The Mirror prompt asks you to select the objects you want to mirror. Select the lines in your drawing that you would like to mirror (we selected the left rectangle in the example to the left). When you are finished selecting lines to mirror, press **ENTER**.
- **Step 1**: The Mirror prompt asks you for the first point of your mirror line. (In our example, the mirror line is represented as a dashed line. This line does not always exist in your drawing.) **CLICK ONCE** to the right of the rectangle.
- **Step 2**: The Mirror prompt asks you for the second point of your mirror line. Turn Ortho on by pressing the **F8** key. Drag the AutoCAD cursor downward and **CLICK ONCE**.
- The Mirror prompt asks if you would like to delete the source objects (it is really asking if you want to delete the original rectangle). Type the letter **N** (for no) on the keyboard and press **ENTER**.

Examples of Mirrored Lines

- The mirror is extremely useful when working on floor plans and elevations. It allows you to duplicate large portions of your drawing without having to re-draw them.

- When you mirror a line or group of lines you can choose to delete or keep the original objects.

Stretch

Use **STRETCH** to select endpoints and move their location in your drawing. The lines that are connected to those endpoints are automatically adjusted.

Stretching Lines in Your Drawing

The Stretch command requires that you draw a **CROSSING SELECTION** around the endpoints that you want to change. The remaining endpoints in your drawing remain unchanged.

- Type the command **STRETCH** and press **ENTER**.
- The stretch prompt asks you to select the objects to stretch (it is really asking you to draw a crossing window over the endpoints that you want to stretch). Select the lower right endpoint of the rectangle by drawing a **CROSSING WINDOW**.
- **Step 1**: **CLICK ONCE** to the right and below the lower right corner of the rectangle.
- **Step 2**: **CLICK ONCE** to the left and above the lower right corner of the rectangle and press **ENTER**.
- **Step 3**: The stretch prompt asks you for the base point of your stretch. **ENDPOINT** snap to the lower right corner of the rectangle.
- **Step 4**: The stretch prompt asks you for the second point of your stretch. Drag the AutoCAD cursor to the location on the screen where you want the lower right corner of the new stretched shape and **CLICK ONCE**.

- Try using Ortho (Click **ORTHO** button or press **F8**) to stretch the same rectangle, as indicated in the diagrams to the left.

- Notice the difference between stretching the bottom right corner and stretching the bottom right and top right corners.

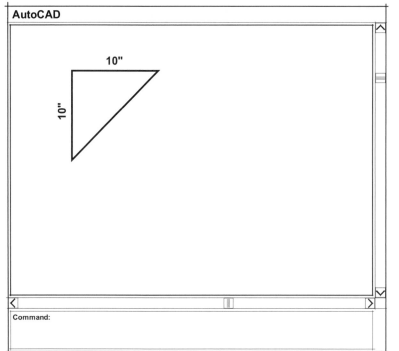

Learning Exercise

Using the commands discussed in Chapters 1–3, draw and edit the sketches to the left. There are additional exercises available for download at books.dougseidler.com.

· Set your drawing units to architectural (feet and inches.)

· Draw a triangle with a left and top side 10" long.

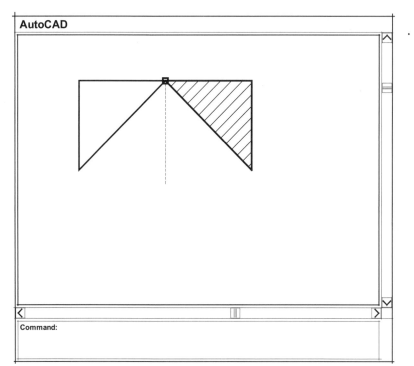

· **MIRROR** the triangle about the top right **END-POINT**.

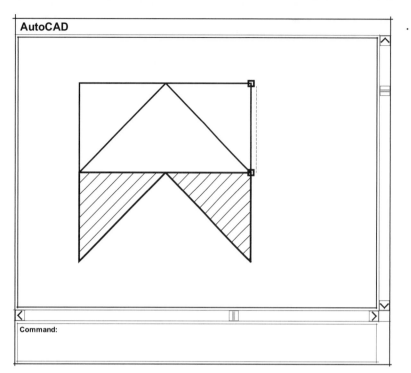

- **COPY** the two triangles down **10"**.

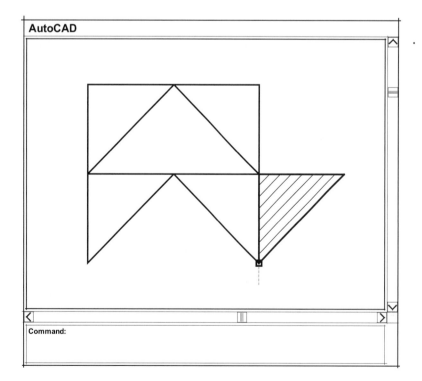

- **MIRROR** the bottom right triangle about the bottom right **ENDPOINT**.

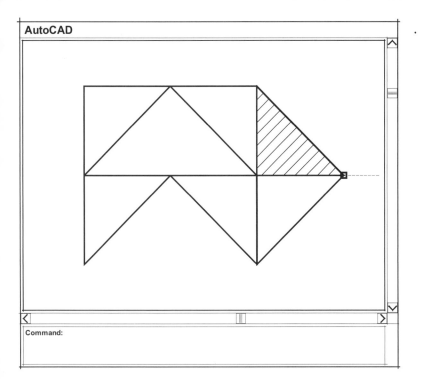

· **MIRROR** the bottom right triangle about the top right **ENDPOINT**.

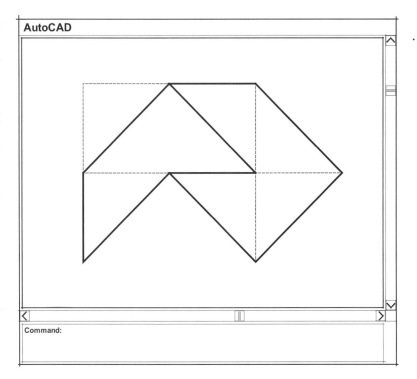

· **ERASE** the dashed lines.

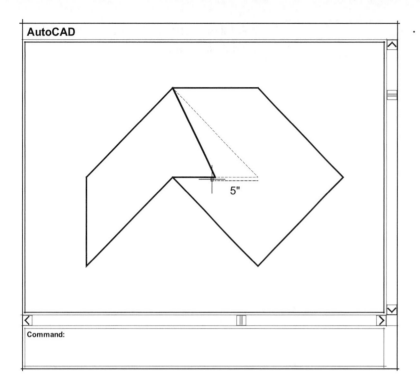

- **STRETCH** the indicated endpoint **5"** to the left.

CHAPTER 4
Drawing with Accuracy and Speed

In the previous three chapters you learned the AutoCAD equivalent to many of the skills you already possess from your experience with manual drawing. The concepts and commands in this chapter will be new to you if you have not previously used a digital drawing program. That said, you will use the commands introduced in this chapter more frequently than any of the other commands discussed in this book.

Consider the following questions as you work through this chapter:
· How can the concepts and commands in this chapter help me draw more efficiently?
· Many of the commands in this chapter involve a combination of multiple manual drawing skills. What manual drawing skills would you combine to achieve the same result as the commands discussed in this chapter?

Polyline

A polyline is really just a series of connected lines that are grouped together. This means that when you select any single segment within a polyline, AutoCAD will select the entire polyline. You will find many instances when polylines increase your drawing efficiency (some by the end of this chapter).

· Drawing with the Polyline command (**PLINE**) is the exact same as drawing with the Line command. The resulting lines look and behave the same, with the single exception that they are joined together.

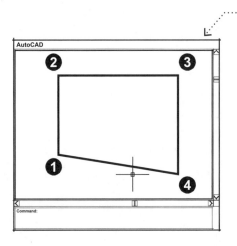

· Type the command **PLINE** and press **ENTER**.
· **Step 1**: Using the mouse, **CLICK ONCE** in the lower left of the AutoCAD drawing area.
· **Steps 2–4**: **CLICK ONCE** in the AutoCAD drawing area, following the diagram on the left.
· Type **CLOSE** and press **ENTER** on the keyboard to end the Polyline command and to close your shape.

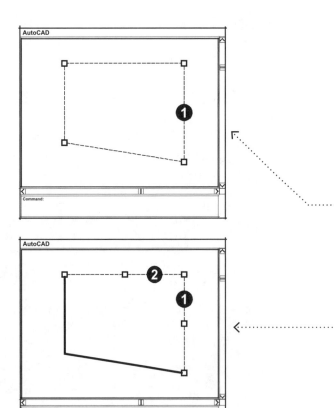

Grips

· The blue squares at the endpoints and mid-points of lines are called grips. These grips show up when you select a line or shape before you start a command (e.g., move, copy, or erase).
· By clicking on a grip, you can stretch the selected object.

More About Polylines

· When you select a single line segment in a polyline, the entire polyline is selected.

· Polylines have grips only at the endpoints of line segments.

More About Lines

· When you select a single line segment in a series of lines, only the individually selected line is highlighted.

· Lines have grips at the endpoints and the midpoints of line segments.

Editing Polylines

The **PEDIT** command allows you to change the width of polylines, convert lines to polylines, and join lines to an existing polyline. Although there are more options available in the **PEDIT** command, we will focus on the three most used commands.

Changing Lines to Polylines	Joining Lines to a Polyline	Changing the Width of a Polyline

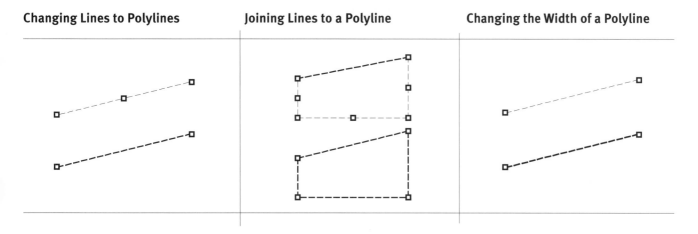

Changing Lines to Polylines

- Type the command **PEDIT** and press **ENTER**.
- Select a single line in your drawing that you would like to convert to a polyline (AutoCAD will allow you to select only one line).
- The **PEDIT** prompt asks you if you would like to turn the selected line into a polyline. Type the letter **Y** (for yes) and press **ENTER**.
- Press **ENTER** or **ESCAPE** to exit the **PEDIT COMMAND**.

Joining Lines to a Polyline

- Type the command **PEDIT** and press **ENTER**.
- **SELECT** a single line or polyline in your drawing (AutoCAD will allow you to select only one line).
- If you selected a line, the **PEDIT** prompt asks you if you would like to turn the selected line into a polyline. Type the letter **Y** (for yes) and press **ENTER**.
- Type the letter **J** and press **ENTER** to start the **JOIN** portion of the **PEDIT** command.
- **SELECT** the lines you would like to join to your originally selected line or polyline. Press **ENTER** when you have finished selecting lines. Note: AutoCAD will join only lines that share endpoints.
- Press **ENTER** or **ESCAPE** to exit the **PEDIT** command.

Changing the Width of a Polyline

- Type the command **PEDIT** and press **ENTER**.
- Select a single line or polyline in your drawing.
- If you selected a line, the **PEDIT** prompt asks you if you would like to turn the selected line into a polyline. Type the letter **Y** (for yes) and press **ENTER**.
- Type the letter **W** and press **ENTER** to start the **WIDTH** portion of the **PEDIT** command.
- Type a new width on the keyboard (i.e., **2"**) and press **ENTER**.
- Press **ENTER** or **ESCAPE** to exit the **PEDIT** command.

- Setting the width of a polyline to **0** will return the line to its original thickness.

- Some people use polyline widths as line weights when drawing plans and sections in AutoCAD. A much easier method for drawing with line weight is discussed in Chapter 5.

Trim

The **TRIM** command allows you to precisely trim the end of a line, polyline, circle, or arc based on its intersection with a second line (or cutting edge).

- Type the command **TRIM** and press **ENTER**.
- **Step 1: CLICK ONCE** on the line, polyline, arc, or circle that you want to use as a cutting edge and press **ENTER**.
- **Step 2: CLICK ONCE** on the first line that you want to trim. AutoCAD will erase the portion of that line that extends beyond the cutting edge.
- **Step 3: CLICK ONCE** on the second line that you want to trim.
- Press **ENTER** or **ESCAPE** to exit the **TRIM** command.

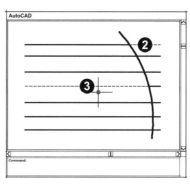

Controlling the Trim

- When you click on a line that you want to trim, AutoCAD will trim relative to the cutting edge. You are telling AutoCAD which part of the line you want to trim or erase.

Trimming Multiple Lines

- You can draw a **CROSSING SELECTION** over a series of lines to trim them all at once. This is quicker than individually selecting the lines that you want to trim.

Extend

The **EXTEND** command allows you to precisely extend the end of a line, polyline, circle, or arc based on its intersection with a second line (or projection edge).

- Type the command **EXTEND** and press **ENTER**.
- **Step 1**: **CLICK ONCE** on the line, polyline, arc, or circle that you want to use as a projection edge and press **ENTER**.
- **Step 2**: **CLICK ONCE** on the first line that you want to extend. AutoCAD will extend that line to the projection edge.
- **Step 3**: **CLICK ONCE** on the second line that you want to extend.
- Press **ENTER** or **ESCAPE** to exit the **EXTEND** command.

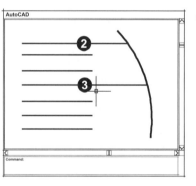

Controlling the Extend

- AutoCAD allows you to extend a line in two directions. Click on the side of the midpoint in the direction that you would like to extend.

Extending Multiple Lines

- You can draw a **CROSSING SELECTION** over a series of lines to extend them all at once. This is quicker than individually selecting the lines that you want to extend.

Offset

The **OFFSET** command creates a parallel line or a concentric circle a set distance from an existing line, arc, or circle. This command is mostly used to set the thickness of walls in floor plans.

Offsetting Lines

- Type the command **OFFSET** and press **ENTER**.
- Type the distance you want to offset lines (e.g., **6"**) and press **ENTER**.
- **Step 1**: **CLICK ONCE** on the line, polyline, arc, or circle that you want to offset.
- **Step 2**: **CLICK ONCE** on the side of the line where you want to create the parallel line.
- AutoCAD allows you to offset multiple objects without restarting the **OFFSET** command. Press **ENTER** or **ESCAPE** to exit the **OFFSET** command.

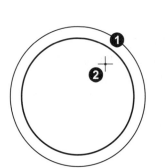

- AutoCAD will remember your last offset distance when you start the **OFFSET** command. If you want to keep this distance you can press **ENTER** rather than entering the distance again.

- You can draw an entire floor plan with Line, Offset, Trim, and Extend.

Fillet

The **FILLET** command is a combination of the Trim and Extend commands. It will extend two lines to their exact intersection and trim the portions of the line that are beyond the intersection.

· Type the command **FILLET** and press **ENTER**.
· **Step 1**: **CLICK ONCE** on the first line that you want to connect.
· **Step 2**: **CLICK ONCE** on the second line that you want to connect.

· The fillet command automatically ends after you select the second line. You can press the **SPACEBAR** or **ENTER** key to repeat the **FILLET** command.

· Notice the relationship between the point where you select a line and the portion of the line that AutoCAD keeps when filleting two lines.

· You can fillet two lines, arcs, or polylines.

Radius Fillet

Setting a **RADIUS** in the Fillet command will provide a curved or radius connection between the lines.

· Type the command **FILLET** and press **ENTER**.
· Type the letter **R** (for radius) and press **ENTER**. Enter the value of the radius (e.g., **5"**) and press **ENTER**.
· **Step 1**: **CLICK ONCE** on the first line that you want to connect.
· **Step 2**: **CLICK ONCE** on the second line that you want to connect.

· The Fillet command remembers the previously set radius. Set the **RADIUS** back to **0** when you want a non-radius fillet.

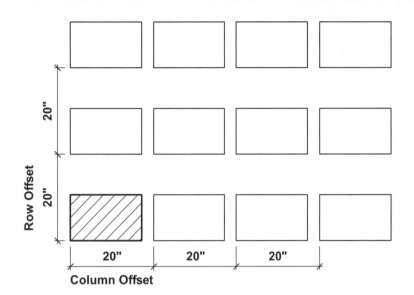

Rectangular Array

The rectangular array command allows you to quickly create duplicates of an original object in a grid pattern.

· In the example to the left, the shaded rectangle was duplicated using the rectangular array command.
· There are **3 ROWS** and **4 COLUMNS**.
· Both the **ROW OFFSET** and **COLUMN OFFSET** are **20"**.

· Type the command **ARRAY** and press **ENTER**.

· Select the **RECTANGULAR ARRAY** option at the top of the dialog box.

· **CLICK ONCE** on the **SELECT OBJECTS** button. The dialog box will disappear, and AutoCAD will prompt you to select the object you want to include in your array. When you have selected this object, press **ENTER**.

· Input the number of **ROWS** and **COLUMNS** for your array. Rows are horizontal. Columns are vertical.

· Input the **ROW OFFSET** and **COLUMN OFFSET** for your array. Positive distances for **ROWS** (e.g., **20"**) are in the up direction. Positive distances for **COLUMNS** (e.g., **20"**) are in the right direction.

· Press the **PREVIEW** button to preview your array in your drawing. If you are satisfied, **CLICK ONCE** on the **ACCEPT** button. If you want to make changes, **CLICK ONCE** on the **MODIFY** button.

Array

⦿ Rectangular Array   ○ Polar Array   Select Objects

Rows [＿＿]   Columns [＿＿]   12 Objects Selected

Row Offset: [＿＿]
Collumn Offset: [＿＿]
Angle of Array [＿＿]

OK
Cancel
Preview <

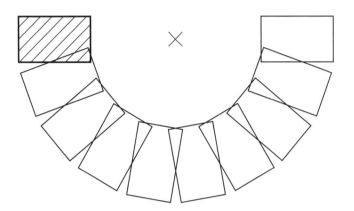

Polar Array

The Polar Array command allows you to quickly create duplicates of an original object in a radial pattern.

· In the example to the left, the shaded rectangle was duplicated using the polar array command.
· There are **10 ITEMS** filling **180 DEGREES**.
· **ROTATE ITEMS AS COPIED** is selected.

· Type the command **ARRAY** and press **ENTER**.

· Select the **POLAR ARRAY** option at the top of the dialog box.

· **CLICK ONCE** on the **SELECT OBJECTS** button. The dialog box will disappear and AutoCAD will prompt you to select the object you want to include in your array. When you have selected the object, press **ENTER**.

· **CLICK ONCE** on the **CENTER POINT** button. The dialog box will disappear and AutoCAD will prompt you to select the center point of rotation for the array.

· Select the array **METHOD** and complete the required fields. (These requirements change depending on the method of array you select.) Positive degrees for **ROTATION** (e.g., **180**) are counterclockwise. Negative degrees for **ROTATION** (e.g., **-180**) are clockwise.

· Press the **PREVIEW** button to preview your array in your drawing. If you are satisfied, **CLICK ONCE** on the **ACCEPT** button. If you want to make changes, **CLICK ONCE** on the **MODIFY** button.

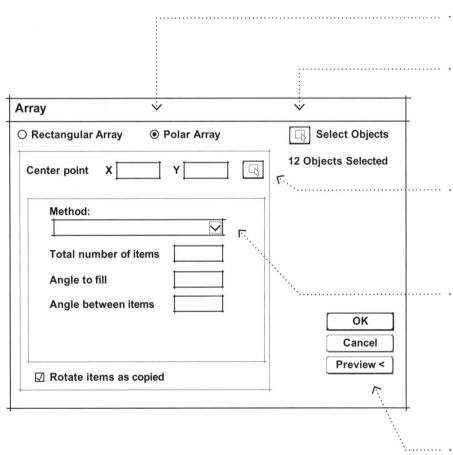

Array

○ Rectangular Array ⊙ Polar Array   ▢ Select Objects

12 Objects Selected

Center point   X [   ] Y [   ]   ▢

Method:
[▽]

Total number of items [   ]

Angle to fill [   ]

Angle between items [   ]

[OK]
[Cancel]
[Preview <]

☑ Rotate items as copied

Break

The Break command splits a single line into two separate lines.

- Type the command **BREAK** and press **ENTER**.
- **Step 1: CLICK ONCE** on the line that you want to break. (This point will be one edge of the break in the line.)
- **Step 2: CLICK ONCE** on the line where you want the second edge of the break.

Alternate Break Method

You can break a line into two lines without introducing a gap between the lines.

- Type the command **BREAK** and press **ENTER**.
- **CLICK ONCE** on the line that you want to break.
- Instead of clicking for the second point of the break, type the character **@** and press **ENTER**.

- AutoCAD will break the line into two lines at the point where you first clicked on the line.

Explode

You can explode a rectangle or polyline into a series of lines. The Explode command will separate a set of lines into individual lines. This command should be used with caution.

- Type the command **EXPLODE** and press **ENTER**.
- **CLICK ONCE** on the polyline or rectangle that you want to explode.
- Press the **ENTER** key to complete the command.

AutoCAD

30"

15"

Command:

AutoCAD

20"

5"

Command:

Learning Exercise

Using the commands discussed in this and previous chapters, draw and edit the sketches to the left. There are additional exercises available for download at http://fairchildbooks.com/book.cms?bookId=179

· Set your drawing units to architectural (feet and inches).

· Draw a horizontal line **30"** in length and a vertical line **15"** in length.

· **OFFSET** the vertical line in **5"** increments to the left.

· **OFFSET** the horizontal line **20"**.

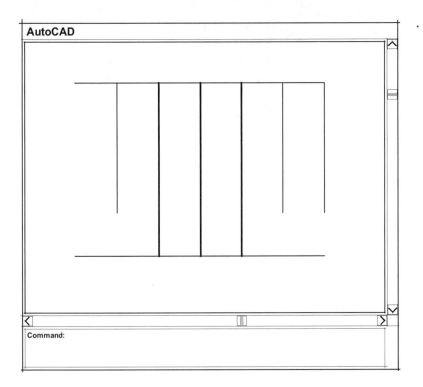

· **EXTEND** the three lines shown in the sketch to the left.

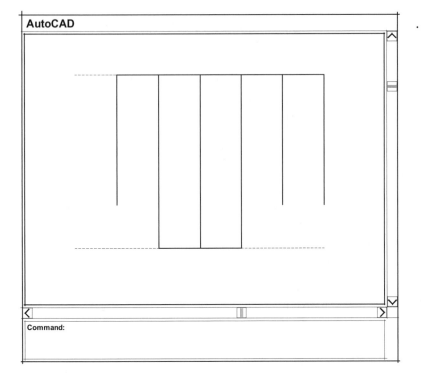

· **TRIM** the dashed lines shown in the sketch to the left.

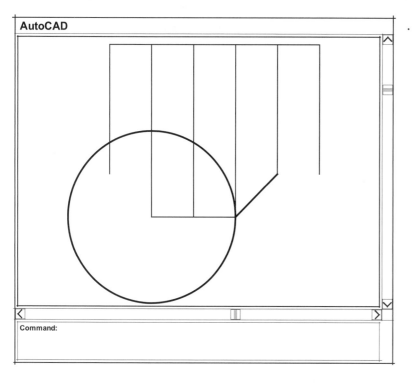

AutoCAD

Command:

· Draw the **CIRCLE** and angled **LINE** using **OBJECT SNAPS**.

AutoCAD

Command:

· **TRIM** the dashed lines shown in the sketch to the left.
· **EXTEND** the diagonal line to the left, as shown in the sketch.

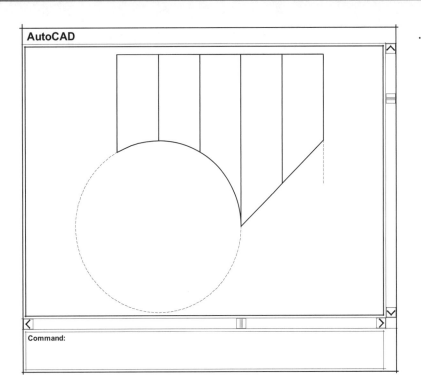

· **TRIM** the dashed line and circle shown in the sketch to the left.

DESIGN
DRAWINGS

CHAPTER 5
Organizing Plans, Sections, and Elevations

In the previous four chapters you were introduced to all the technical tools you need to successfully complete drawings in AutoCAD. In this chapter we look at drawing fundamentals that will turn your AutoCAD drawings into design drawings. These skills include line weight, drawing presentation, and drawing organization.

Consider the following questions as you work through this chapter:

· How can layers help you organize your drawings?
· How can layers help you control line weight in your drawings?
· What are the different ways layers are used in plan, section, and elevation drawings?

Line Weight

Clear and legible line weight will communicate your design better than any combination of AutoCAD commands. You have most likely been introduced to line weight in a manual drafting studio, conceptual drawing studio, or design studio. These drawing conventions existed long before AutoCAD. It is important to understand how to draw in AutoCAD using these conventions.

- When drafting by hand, you adjust your line thickness by adjusting the type of lead in your pencil or by adjusting the pressure applied to the paper.
- In AutoCAD, you adjust line thickness by selecting different colors for different kinds of lines.

Red (Color 1) ———————————

Yellow (Color 2) ———————————

Green (Color 3) ———————————

Cyan (Color 4) ———————————

Blue (Color 5) ———————————

Magenta (Color 6) ———————————

White (Color 7) ———————————

Dark Grey (Color 8) ———————————

Light Grey (Color 9) ———————————

HIDDEN2 (Color 5) — — — — — — — —

CENTER2 (Color 5) —— — —— — —— — ——

Heavy Lines

- These lines are used to delineate objects (in plan or section) that are cut through.
- In AutoCAD use Red (Color 1), Yellow (Color 2), or Green (Color 3).

Medium and Light Lines

- These lines are used to delineate a change in plane or a corner (in elevation).
- In a floor plan, these lines can represent furniture or casework.
- In AutoCAD use Cyan (Color 4) or Blue (Color 5).

Light Lines

- These lines are used to delineate a change in color, material, or surface.
- In a floor plan, these lines can represent a transition from carpeting to wood flooring. In elevation, these lines can represent crown molding or trim around a door.
- In AutoCAD use Magenta (Color 6) or White (Color 7).

Very Light Lines

- These lines are used to delineate surface texture or material patterns.
- In a floor plan, these lines can represent a wood or tile floor material.
- In AutoCAD use Dark Gray (Color 8) or Light Gray (Color 9).

Hidden and Center Line Types

- Hidden lines are used to delineate major objects that are above the floor cutting plane or objects that are hidden behind other objects in your drawing. In AutoCAD, use line type **HIDDEN2**.

- Center lines are used to delineate the centerline of objects like doors, windows, or building structure. In AutoCAD, use line type **CENTER2**.

Selecting Colors in AutoCAD

In AutoCAD, you adjust line thickness by selecting different colors for different kinds of lines. The Select Color dialog box is the primary place you will select colors in AutoCAD.

- AutoCAD recognizes 255 colors. Each of these colors is a potentially different line weight. As you have seen on the previous page, you will use only nine different colors.

The AutoCAD Color Index is separated into sections.

- **COLOR 10** to **COLOR 249** are represented in this section. Disregard these colors when drawing in AutoCAD.

- **COLOR 1** to **COLOR 9** are represented in this section. From left to right, you can click on the desired color in this section to correspond to the different line weights on the previous page.

- **COLOR 250** to **COLOR 255** are represented in this section. These colors will produce various shades of gray when used with solid hatches.

- You can type the color name or number directly into the color input box. The color in this input box will also automatically populate when you select a color by clicking directly on the color swatch.

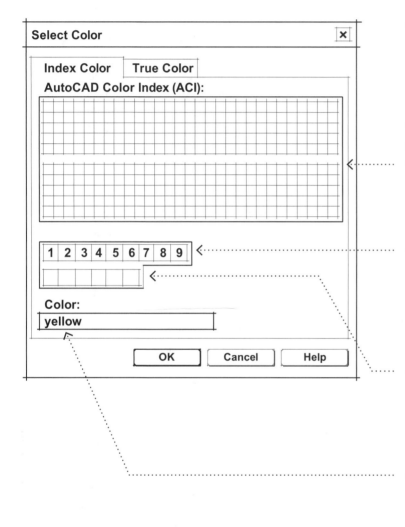

Select Color

Index Color | **True Color**

AutoCAD Color Index (ACI):

1 2 3 4 5 6 7 8 9

Color:
yellow

OK | Cancel | Help

90% Grey	75% Grey	50% Grey	25% Grey	10% Grey
Color 250	Color 251	Color 252	Color 253	Color 254

Hatch Solids
- **COLO R 250** through **COLOR 254** print as different values of gray and are used for solid poché.
- Hatching is discussed in Chapter 8.

Drawing with Layers

Layers serve three primary purposes in AutoCAD.

· **Line Weight** – Lines inherit their **COLOR** and **LINETYPE** from the layer on which they are drawn. You can quickly change the color of all the lines on the furniture layer if you want the furniture to print lighter.

· **Organization** – Layers help categorize and organize lines based on what they represent in your drawings (e.g., doors, walls, etc.).

· **Visibility** – You can turn off layers to print different versions of your floor plan.

Layer Properties Manager

The Layer Properties Manager allows you to set up and modify all the layers in your drawing.

· Type the command **LAYER** and press **ENTER** to open the Layer Properties Manager.

· The **NEW LAYER** button creates a new layer in your drawing.

· The **DELETE LAYER** button will delete the currently selected layer. You cannot delete layers that have lines on them.

· The **SET CURRENT** button will set the selected layer to current. All new lines are drawn on the layer set to current.

· **Name** – **CLICK ONCE** on the layer name to rename the layer.

· **On** – **CLICK ONCE** on the light bulb icon to turn the layer **ON** or **OFF**.

· **Freeze** – **CLICK ONCE** on the sunshine/snowflake icon to **THAW** or **FREEZE** the layer. Objects on locked layers are not visible and cannot be modified.

· **Lock** – **CLICK ONCE** on the lock bulb icon to **LOCK** or **UNLOCK** the layer. Objects on locked layers are visible but cannot be modified.

· **Plot/No Plot** – **CLICK ONCE** on the printer icon to modify if the selected layer will print.

· **Line type** – **CLICK ONCE** on the line type to modify the line type for all objects on that layer.

· **Color** – **CLICK ONCE** on the color swatch to modify the color for all objects on that layer. Use Colors 1 through 9 for lines and Colors 250 through 254 for solid hatches.

Properties Button Bar

The properties button bar is located at the top of the AutoCAD screen. This bar allows you to modify the properties for any object in Auto-CAD (including line color and line type).

· Good AutoCAD drawings assign properties to layers, not individual objects (or lines).
· It is tempting to change the color of lines in your drawing using the properties button bar. You will save time later in your project if you create and use layers to control the color of lines in your drawing.
· In your drawing, 99 percent of the objects should have ByLayer assignments for color and line type. (This means the objects get their color and line type from their layer.)

Layers Button Bar

The Layers button bar is located at the top of the AutoCAD screen. This bar allows you to move any object in AutoCAD to a specific layer.

Setting the Current Layer

The layer displayed in the Layers button bar is the current layer. Any objects drawn in AutoCAD will be automatically placed on this layer.

· The current layer in this example is **A-WALL**.
· You can change the current layer by clicking the down arrow to the right of the current layer and selecting the desired layer.

Changing an Object's Layers

It is easy to change an object to a new layer.

· Select a line in your drawing. The layer displayed in the Layers button bar will change to the layer assigned to the line you selected.
· You can change the object's layer by clicking the down arrow to the right of the current layer and selecting the desired layer.
· Press the **ESCAPE** key twice to deselect the object and continue drawing.

Floor Plans

Floor plans are a horizontal section taken through a house or building. They are usually cut 3'–6' above the floor but may vary according to the project. This imaginary line is referred to as the cutting plane.

· This horizontal plane slices through walls, doors, windows, and columns. Below the slice, we see furniture, flooring material, countertops, and so on.

· When drawing a floor plan in AutoCAD, you will categorize lines based on what they represent in your drawing and based on their relative thickness.

· The scale of the drawing will determine the appropriate number of line weights. A floor plan drawn at 1/4" = 1'-0" only needs four different line weights.

· There may be different layers in your AutoCAD drawing that have the same color. For example, the furniture layer and the countertop layer may share the same color because you want them to print with the same line weight.

Typical Floor Plan Layers

The following represents typical floor plan layers and appropriate layer colors. Many offices set their own office standards for layer names and layer colors.

· Understanding the concepts illustrated below will allow you to adapt to any office environment.

Very Light Lines

· **A-Floor-Hatch:** Color 8 or Color 9.
  These lines typically represent material patterns or scale of material. This should not visually distract from the overall drawing.

Medium Lines

· **A-Door:** Color 3 or Color 4.
  The number of lines drawn is determined by the scale of the drawing. (Refer to page 62 for examples of doors drawn at different scales.)

· **A-Window:** Color 3 or Color 4.
  The number of lines drawn is determined by the scale of the drawing. (Refer to page 63 for examples of windows drawn at different scales.)

· **A-Furn:** Color 5 or Color 6.
  The abbreviation **FURN** is short for furniture.

· **A-Case:** Color 5 or Color 6.
  The abbreviation **CASE** is short for casework. This layer can include cabinets and built-ins.

Heavy Lines

· **A-Wall:** Color 1 or Color 2.
  Some designers prefer to draw interior and exterior walls with different line weights.
  A-Wall-Intr: Color 2 (interior walls).
  A-Wall-Extr: Color 1 (exterior walls).

The Plan Cut and Line Weight

When drawing floor plans, you need to clearly identify the difference between solid mass (or walls) and void (or rooms).

- The right side of this floor plan was drawn with a single line weight and does not emphasize the horizontal section cut. In this drawing, it is difficult to identify space.

- The left side of this floor plan was drawn with a hierarchy of lines to convey the spatial properties of this church. In this drawing, the contrast between mass and void is clearer than in the previous drawing.

Poché

Solid tone can be added to a drawing to add contrast between the mass and the void. In AutoCAD you can add poché with the hatch command, which is discussed in Chapter 8.

· The left side of this floor plan uses a solid tone to communicate space by creating contrast between the walls and the space of this church. The tone in this drawing is a solid hatch pattern and is Color 252.

· The right side of this floor plan uses multiple angled lines to communicate space by creating contrast between the walls and the space of this church. The tone in this drawing is an ANSI31 hatch pattern and is Color 9.

Il Redentore, Venice, Italy, begun 1576, Andrea Palladio
drawing by Kristine Mortensen.

Quantity Not Quality

When you draw by hand, the detail you include in your drawing is limited by the scale of the drawing. A 1/16" = 1'-0" floor plan is too small for you to draw a doorjamb. However, a 1/2" = 1'-0" enlargement of the same floor plan is large enough to show a doorjamb.

AutoCAD makes it easy to zoom in closer to the doorjamb and include precise detail without regard for the scale of the drawing. However, it is important to apply hand-drafting logic to drawings created in AutoCAD. Include the appropriate number of lines (or detail) based on the scale of your drawing.

	Layer Name	Layer Color
1/16" = 1'-0"	A-DOOR	CYAN (4)
	A-WALL	YELLOW (2)
1/8" = 1'-0"	A-DOOR	CYAN (4)
	A-WALL	RED (1)
1/4" = 1'-0"	A-DOOR	CYAN (4)
	A-DOOR-JAMB	YELLOW (2)
	A-WALL	RED (1)
1/2" = 1'-0"	A-DOOR	CYAN (4)
	A-DOOR-JAMB	YELLOW (2)
	A-WALL	RED (1)

As stated, AutoCAD makes it easy to zoom in closer to the doorjamb and include precise detail without regard for the scale of the drawing. Care should be taken not to add too much detail that will clutter the drawing. Notice the extra information drawn in the larger scale plans.

Layer Name	Layer Color
A-GLAZ	GREEN (3)
A-WALL	YELLOW (2)
A-GLAZ-SILL	WHITE (7)
A-GLAZ-MULL	WHITE (7)
A-GLAZ	GREEN (3)
A-WALL	RED (1)
A-GLAZ-SILL	WHITE (7)
A-GLAZ-MULL	MAGENTA (6)
A-GLAZ	GREEN (3)
A-WALL	RED (1)
A-GLAZ-SILL	WHITE (7)
A-GLAZ-MULL	MAGENTA (6)
A-GLAZ	GREEN (3)
A-WALL	RED (1)

1/16" = 1'-0"

1/8" = 1'-0"

1/4" = 1'-0"

1/2" = 1'-0"

Building Sections

Building sections are vertical slices through a house or building. They are usually cut through the entire building but may vary according to the project. This imaginary line is referred to as the cutting plane.

· This vertical plane slices through walls and windows. Building sections should not be cut through columns. Beyond the slice, we see wall openings, windows, doors, wall material, and so on.

· When drawing a building section in AutoCAD, you will categorize lines based on their relative thickness.

· The scale of the drawing will determine the appropriate number of line weights. A section drawn at 1/4"=1'-0" only needs four different line weights.

Typical Building Section Layers

The following represents typical section layers and appropriate layer colors. Many offices set their own office standards for layer names and layer colors.

·   Understanding the concepts illustrated below will allow you to adapt to any office environment.

Very Light Lines

·   **A-Sect-XLight:** Color 8 or Color 9.
These lines typically represent material patterns or scale of material. These lines should not visually distract from the overall drawing.

Light Lines

·   **A-Sect-Light:** Color 6 or Color 7.
These lines typically represent a change in material on a wall or surface. This can include wood trim around a door or opening.

Medium Lines

·   **A-Sect-Medium:** Color 4 or Color 5.
These lines are used to delineate a change in plane, a corner in elevation, or an opening in a wall. They are also referred to as profile lines.

Heavy Lines

·   **A-Sect-Dark:** Color 1 or Color 2.
These lines are used to delineate objects that are being sliced through, including walls and windows.

·   **A-Sect-Floor:** Color 1.
Some designers add a separate layer to draw the floor or ground in section. The ground layer should be as dark or darker than the darkest line in your drawing.

Section Cut and Line Weight

Just like the floor plan, when drawing sections you need to clearly identify the difference between solid mass (or walls) and void (or space).

· The building section above was drawn with a single line weight and does not emphasize the section cut. In this drawing it is difficult to identify space.

Rachofsky House, Dallas, TX, 1991–96, Richard Meier
drawing by Lori Anderson Wier. Reprinted with permission
of Richard Meier & Partners Architects LLP.

· The building section above was drawn with a hierarchy of lines to convey the spatial properties of this house. In this drawing, the contrast between mass and void is clearer than in the previous drawing.

Poché

Solid tone can be added to a drawing to show contrast between the mass and the void. In AutoCAD you can add poché with the Hatch command, which is discussed in Chapter 8.

· The building section above uses a solid tone to communicate the space inside this home. The tone in this drawing is a solid hatch pattern and is Color 252.

· The building section above uses multiple angled lines to communicate the space inside this home. The tone in this drawing is an ANSI31 hatch pattern and is Color 9.

Building Elevations and Interior Elevations

Unlike sections, elevations do not require that we cut through the building or house. Elevations are two-dimensional drawings that describe what surfaces will look like after the project is built.

- Interior elevations usually describe a single wall in a room (Preferred scale: 1/4"=1'-0").
- Exterior (or Building) Elevations usually describe a single side of the building (Preferred scale: 1/4"=1'-0" or 1/8" = 1'-0").

- When drawing an elevation in AutoCAD we will categorize lines based on their relative thickness.

- The scale of the drawing will determine the appropriate number of line weights. An elevation drawn at 1/4" = 1'-0" only needs four distinct line weights.

Typical Elevation Layers

The following represents typical elevation layers and appropriate layer colors. Many offices set their own office standards for layer names and layer colors.

· Understanding the concepts illustrated below will allow you to adapt to any office environment.

Very Light Lines

· **A-Elev-XLight:** Color 8 or Color 9.
These lines typically represent material patterns or scale of material. These lines should not visually distract the overall drawing.

Light Lines

· **A-Elev-Light:** Color 6 or Color 7.
These lines typically represent a change in material on a wall or surface. This can include wood trim around a door or opening.

Medium Lines

· **A-Elev-Medium:** Color 4 or Color 5.
These lines are used to delineate a change in plane, a corner in elevation, or an opening in a wall. They are also referred to as profile lines.

Heavy Lines

· **A-Elev-Dark:** Color 1 or Color 2.
These lines are used to delineate the perimeter of the elevation.

· **A-Elev-Floor:** Color 1.
Some designers add a separate layer to draw the floor or ground in their elevations. The ground layer should be as dark as or darker than the darkest line in your drawing.

Elevation Line Weight

When drawing elevations you need to clearly indicate the difference between lines that identify a change in plane and lines that identify a change in surface material.

· This elevation was drawn with just a couple of line weights and does not emphasize the edges of surfaces. In this drawing, it is difficult to identify depth.

East Elevation, Rachofsky House, Dallas, TX, 1991–96, Richard Meier drawing by Cheri Kotsiopoulos. Reprinted with permission of Richard Meier & Partners Architects LLP.

· This elevation was drawn with a hierarchy of lines to convey the depth of this house elevation. In this drawing, the contrast between the edges of surfaces and lines that define a change in surface material is clearer than in the previous drawing.

Poché

Solid tone can be added to an elevation to add contrast between the mass and the void or to communicate material. In AutoCAD you can add poché with the Hatch command, which is discussed in Chapter 8.

· This elevation uses a solid tone to communicate material by creating contrast between the walls and the windows of this house. The tone in this drawing is a solid hatch pattern and is Color 253.

· In addition to the tone used in the elevation at the top of this page, this elevation further communicates depth by adding shadow with a solid tone. The shadow tone in this drawing is a solid hatch pattern and is Color 252.

The Interior Elevation/Section and Line Weight

Often, you will use a section/interior elevation to identify both interior finishes and spatial relationship in a design project. Just like the floor plan, you need to clearly identify the difference between solid mass (or walls) and void (or space).

· The section/elevation above was drawn with a single line weight and does not emphasize the section cut or the depth of interior space. In this drawing it is difficult to identify space.

Interior Elevation, Master's Thesis Project, 2006, Lori Anderson Wier, New England School of Art and Design at Suffolk University.

· The section/elevation above was drawn with a hierarchy of lines to convey the spatial properties of this design. In this drawing, the contrast between mass, void, and spatial depth is clearer than in the previous drawing.

Poché

Solid tone can be added to a drawing to show contrast between the mass and the void. In AutoCAD you can add poché with the Hatch command, which is discussed in Chapter 8.

· The section/elevation above uses a solid tone to communicate the space inside this design. The tone in this drawing is a solid hatch pattern and is Color 252.

· The building section above uses multiple angled lines to communicate the space inside this design. The tone in this drawing is an ANSI31 hatch pattern and is Color 9.

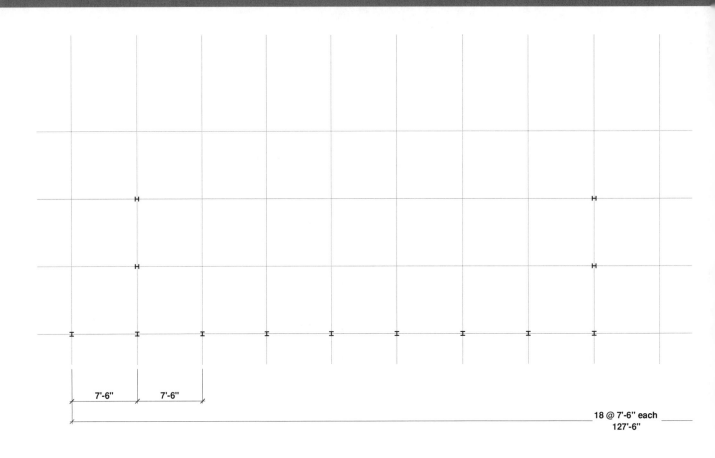

7'-6"   7'-6"

18 @ 7'-6" each
127'-6"

Learning Exercise

Completed in 1949, the Eames House represents one of 25 "Case Study" homes. The Case Study House Program, commissioned by *Arts and Architecture* magazine, challenged architects to design homes that could be built and furnished with building technologies used during World War II.

At the end of this and subsequent chapters, you will complete portions of the Eames House to reinforce concepts discussed during the chapter.

Creating Your Drawing

· Open AutoCAD.
· Save the new drawing as **DDFD-EAMES.DWG**

· Set your drawing units to Architectural (feet and inches).

Creating Your Layers

Create the following layers. You can open the layer manager by typing the command **LAYER** and pressing **ENTER**.

· **S-GRID**   Color 252   NoPlot
· **S-COL**   Color 2
· Set the current layer to **S-GRID**

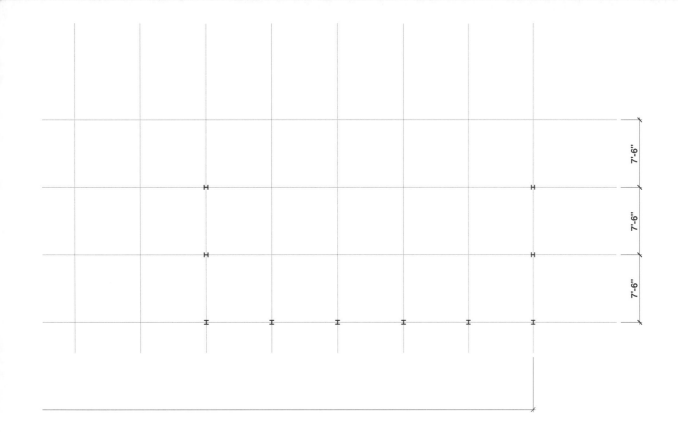

Drawing the Structural Grid

· Draw a horizontal line **140'-0"** in length.

· Offset this horizontal line two times by **7'-6"**.

· Draw a vertical line **36'-0"** in height.

· Use the **OFFSET** or **ARRAY** command to create the remaining vertical lines.

Drawing the Columns

· The structural columns in this house are 5"×5" w-flanges (I beams).
· Draw a 5"×5" square. If you used the rectangle command, explode the rectangle.
· Erase the left and right side of the square and draw a vertical line between the midpoints of the top and bottom edge.

· Use the copy, rotate, and move commands to position the columns to match the drawing above.

· Save your drawing.

Creating Your Layers

Create the following layers.
- **A-GLAZ**   Color 6
- Set the current layer to **A-GLAZ**

Drawing the Exterior Window Panels

- Draw a rectangle **3'–6-1/2"** wide × **3"** tall.

- Draw a second rectangle **7'–1"** wide × **3"** tall.

- Use the copy, rotate, and move commands to position the windows to match the drawing above.

- Save your drawing.

Creating Your Layers

Create the following layers.

- **A-WALL**   Color 2
- Set the current layer to **A-WALL**

Drawing the Exterior Wall Panels

- Draw a rectangle **7'1"** wide × **3"** tall.

- Use the copy, rotate, and move commands to position the exterior windows to match the drawing above.

Drawing the Interior Walls

- The interior walls are 4" thick.

- The retaining wall (top wall in drawing) is 12" thick.

- Draw the interior walls to match the dimensions in the drawing above.

- Save your drawing.

Congratulations, you have completed the learning exercise for this chapter.

CHAPTER 6
Drawing and Printing to Scale

This chapter discusses the process of printing your digital drawing. In AutoCAD, you create and save a separate layout for each sheet that you need to print. This allows you to quickly print your drawings in the future and at a moment's notice.

The concepts discussed in this chapter are the most challenging AutoCAD concepts. The best way to master these concepts (like most things in life) is through practice, trial, and error. When you draw by hand, you know the scale of your drawing before you begin drawing. You use an architectural scale to reduce the drawing proportionally to fit on the sheet of paper.

In AutoCAD you draw everything at full scale or real world scale. The advantage to this new method of working is that you can complete a drawing and then determine what size paper and what scale you want to print your drawing. The disadvantage for new learners is that it can be frustrating to struggle with printing when you know how easy it would be to complete the same drawing by hand.

Consider the following questions as you work through this chapter:
· What do you need to know about a manual drawing before you start to draw?
· What do you need to know about your digital drawing before you set up a layout?

- When drawing by hand you use an architectural scale to draw a reduced drawing at a measurable size.
  (Like 1/8"=1'-0")
- When drawing in AutoCAD you draw at real world size (full scale) and AutoCAD will reduce it to the appropriate scale.

Paper Space versus Model Space

AutoCAD has two different areas that you will use to create scaled drawings.

Model Space

- **MODEL SPACE** (or the Model tab) is the place in AutoCAD where we draft 95 percent of our lines.
- While in Model Space, you draft at true world scale. True world scale means if you are drafting a room that is 30'-6" wide by 20'-0" deep in Model Space you will draft your lines 30'-6" wide by 20'-0" deep.

Paper Space / Layout View

- The **LAYOUT VIEW** (Layout1, Layout2, and Layout3 tabs) is the place in AutoCAD where you set up the sheets you are going to print or plot.
- Anything that you draft in your Layout View will print the same size as you drafted it. Therefore, if you add 1/8" tall text to your layout view, this text will measure 1/8" tall on your printed sheet.

Viewport

- The opening (or window) you see in the Layout View is called a **VIEWPORT**. Viewports allow you to see through your Layout View to the project you drafted in Model Space.

scale factor: 48

scale factor 96

AutoCAD Scale Factors

The Scale Factor concept is unique to Auto-CAD. In the diagram above, the Scale Factor represents the distance between Model Space and the layout view. If you move Model Space farther back, then the drawing in your layout view will get smaller. If you move Model Space closer, then the drawing in your layout view will get larger.

· For a drawing/viewport to be scaled 1/4" = 1'-0", the scale factor is **48.**
· For a drawing/viewport to be scaled 1/8" = 1'-0", the scale factor is **96.**

· As you increase the scale factor, you are increasing the distance between Model Space and Paper Space.

· The farther back you push Model Space, the small your drawing will look in Paper Space (and when printed).

The following is a list of drawing scales and their AutoCAD scale factors:

Drawing Scale	Scale Factor
3"=1'-0"	4
1 1/2"=1'-0"	8
1"=1'-0"	12
3/4"=1'-0"	16
1/2"=1'-0"	24
3/8"=1'-0"	32
1/4"=1'-0"	48
3/16"=1'-0"	64
1/8"=1'-0"	96
3/32"=1'-0"	128
1/16"=1'-0"	192
1/32=1'-0"	384

Plot Styles

When you print a drawing, AutoCAD uses line color to determine the line weight it sends to the printer. The plot style (CTB file) is the file where you set the relationship between line color and line weight.

PLOT STYLE

- When you print a drawing, the CTB file sits between your AutoCAD drawing and the printer. This is the file that communicates to the printer how thick to make each line. For example, the CTB file tells AutoCAD to make all the red lines .0210" thick (about 1/32").

- This book uses a custom plot style that can be installed on any computer.

- The CTB file is installed on AutoCAD and not saved with your drawing. If you are plotting on a new computer or in a new location, you should take this file with you and install it on the new computer. We will help you install a CTB file later in this chapter.

- While there is no national (or international) standard for line weights and colors, it is easy to add additional plot styles to AutoCAD when you need to print drawings created with a different color standard than you use for your projects.

Color Dependent Versus Named Plot Style

There are two different types of plot styles in AutoCAD. While this book will focus on using the color dependent plot style, it is important that you understand what a named plot style is and how to convert it to a color dependent plot style.

· Each AutoCAD drawing can be set up for either a CTB file or an STB file but not both.

Color Dependent Plot Style (CTB file)

· This plot style determines line thickness based solely on the color of the line in your drawing.
. CTB files are the easiest to implement and the most commonly used in offices.

Named Plot Styles (STB)

· Recent versions of AutoCAD have included a new method to plot called **NAMED PLOT STYLES**.
· This plot style determines line thickness based on the layer that the line is drawn on. For example, a line on the door layer will print a specified thickness regardless of its color.
· Because this new method is not widely adopted in the profession, this book will only discuss **COLOR DEPENDENT PLOT STYLE (CTB)**.

CTB FILE

STB FILE

Convert your drawing for CTB plot styles
It is possible that your drawing is set up for named plot styles instead of color dependent plot styles. Symptoms include only seeing **STB** plot styles in the plot style selection box (discussed later in this chapter).
· To convert your drawing to Color Dependent Plot Styles, type **CONVERTPSTYLES** and press **ENTER**.

CTB Files

The following guide will walk you through the process of installing a new **CTB** file on your computer.

DDFD-FULL.CTB

DDFD-HALF.CTB

DDFD-FULL.CTB	DDFD-HALF.CTB
COLOR 1	COLOR 1
COLOR 2	COLOR 2
COLOR 3	COLOR 3
COLOR 4	COLOR 4
COLOR 5	COLOR 5
COLOR 6	COLOR 6
COLOR 7	COLOR 7
COLOR 8	COLOR 8
COLOR 9	COLOR 9

There are two different versions of the CTB file that are compatible with the line colors described in this guide.

· **DDFD-FULL.CTB** is used to print 95 percent of your drawings and will print the line weight at full thickness.

· **DDFD-HALF.CTB** reduces each line weight by 50 percent and is useful when printing a reduced drawing at 11"×17" or 8.5"×11".

· You can download both **CTB** files from our web site: http://www.fairchildbooks.com/book.cms?bookId=179

Installing a New CTB File

· Visit our web site now and download these files to the **MY DOCUMENTS** folder on your computer.

· Open AutoCAD.

· Type the command **STYLESMANAGER** and press **ENTER**.
  This command will open the location on your computer where AutoCAD stores (and looks for) plot styles.

· **DOUBLE CLICK** on the icon labeled **ADD-A-PLOT STYLE TABLE WIZARD**.

· **CLICK ONCE** the **NEXT>** button.

· Select **USE AN EXISTING PLOT STYLE TABLE** and **CLICK ONCE** the **NEXT>** button.

Add Plot Style Table - Browse file name   ✕

Begin	**Select the existing plot style table...**
Table Type	
Browse File	DDFD-FULL.ctb ▽
File Name	[Browse]
Finish	

[< Back]   [Next >]   [Cancel]

- **CLICK ONCE** the **BROWSE** button and locate the **CTB** file you downloaded from our web site.
- **CLICK ONCE** the **NEXT›** button.

Add Plot Style Table - File name   ✕

Begin	**Enter a name for the new plot style table...**
Table Type	
Browse File	File name:
File Name	DDFD-FULL
Finish	

[< Back]   [Next >]   [Cancel]

- Type **DDFD-FULL** in the file name box and **CLICK ONCE** the **NEXT›** button.

Add Plot Style Table - Finish   ✕

Begin	**A plot style table has been created...**
Table Type	
Browse File	
File Name	
Finish	

[< Back]   [Finish]   [Cancel]

- **CLICK ONCE** the **FINISH** button to complete the wizard.

- You have successfully imported a **CTB** file to AutoCAD.
- You can repeat these steps to install **DDFD-HALF.CTB**.

Standard Paper Sizes

When you start a hand drawing you need to know what size paper you are going to use. When you set up a digital drawing for printing, you need to know what paper sizes are available.

Standard Paper Sizes

The following paper sizes are available for most laser and ink jet printers:

· Letter	8½" × 11"	(see tabloid setup)
· Legal	8½" × 14"	(see tabloid setup)
· Tabloid	11" × 17"	pages 89 and 90

Small Format Printers

· Most ink jet and laser printers will print Letter and Legal size paper. Some will also print Tabloid (11" × 17") paper as well.

Large Format Paper Sizes

The following paper sizes are available for most large format printers and plotters:

· ANSI A	8½" × 11"	(see tabloid setup)
· ANSI B	11" × 17"	pages 89 and 90
· ANSI C	17" × 22"	
· ANSI D	22" × 34"	
· ANSI E	34" × 44"	
· ARCH C	18" × 24"	pages 89 and 92
· ARCH D	24" × 36"	pages 89 and 94
· ARCH E	36" × 48"	
· ARCH E1	30" × 42"	

Large Format Printers

· Large format printers (plotters) print a variety of sizes. All allow you to load individual sheets of paper. Some allow you to load a roll of paper.
· When printing to a large format printer, it is important to identify the width of the printer. If the printer is 24" wide then the largest paper you can print on is restricted to 24". You can print on 18" × 24" and 24" × 36" but not 30" × 42".

Creating Layouts

There are several pre-defined layouts available for download at our web site: http://www.fairchildbooks.com/book.cms?bookId=179 The following guide will take you through the process of setting up your own layout.

Setting Your Drawing Units

·   Set your **UNITS** to **ARCHITECTURAL** and your precision to **1/32"**.

Creating Your Layers

Create the following layers. You can open the layer manager by typing the command **LAYER** and pressing **ENTER**.

·   **TB-BORDER**   Color 1
·   **TB-TEXT**   Color 4
·   **TB-VIEWPORT**   Color 31, NoPlot
·   Set the current layer to **TB-BORDER**.

Creating Your First Layout

·   The **MODEL** and **LAYOUT** tabs are located at the bottom of the AutoCAD window. **CLICK ONCE** on the **LAYOUT 1** tab.
·   **RIGHT CLICK** on the **LAYOUT 1** tab and select **RENAME**.
·   Rename the layout to match the drawing sheet you would like to set up. For example, you could rename the layout to **SHEET – 11×17** and click **OK**.
·   If there is a rectangle in your drawing, **ERASE** it. This rectangle is a viewport. We will create a new viewport later in this chapter.

·   You are ready to draw your title block. This chapter has several guides to set up different size title blocks. Refer to the chart on the previous page to determine where each guide starts in this chapter.

11" × 17" – Setting Up a Tabloid-Sized Sheet

This sheet size is most commonly used for construction administration sketches or smaller residential projects. The tabloid and portrait layout both have a 0.5" margin which is compatible with most laser and inkjet printers.

11" x 17" Sheet with .5" margin

Portrait Layout

· Set the current layer to **TB-BORDER.**
· Using the **RECTANGLE** command, draw a rect-angle that is **11"** wide and **17"** tall.
· **OFFSET** the rectangle **0.5"** to the inside. This new rectangle represents the margins required by your printer. (With most printers, you cannot print to the edge of the paper.)
· **ERASE** the first **RECTANGLE**. (You do not need this rectangle anymore.)
· Complete your title sheet so it matches the image to the left.

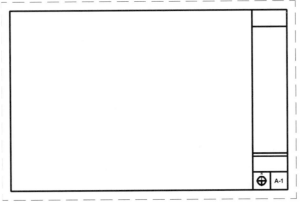

11" x 17" Sheet with .5" margin

Landscape Layout

· Set the current layer to **TB-BORDER**
· Using the rectangle command, draw a **RECTANGLE** that is **17"** wide and **11"** tall.
· **OFFSET** the rectangle **0.5"** to the inside. This new rectangle represents the margins required by your printer. (With most printers, you cannot print to the edge of the paper.)
· **ERASE** the first **RECTANGLE**. (You do not need this rectangle anymore.)
· Complete your title sheet so it matches the image to the left.

Set Up Your Page to Print

The **PAGE SETUP MANAGER** allows you to specify page layout and plotting device settings for each layout in your drawing. The page setup settings that you specify are stored within the layout, making it easy for you to print.

- From the **FILE** menu, select **PAGE SETUP MANAGER**.
- Click once on ***SHEET – 11×17*** (your sheet may have a different name).
- Click the **MODIFY** button.

Follow the steps below to complete the setup for your layout.

Printer / Plotter
- Select the printer you want use for this drawing. Printers installed on your computer are available for selection.

Paper Size
- This selection box will show paper sizes that are available for the printer you selected. Select **TABLOID** or **ANSI B**.

Plot Area
- This selection box allows you to customize what you want AutoCAD to print. Select **EXTENTS**.

Plot Offsets
- Place a checkmark in the **CENTER THE PLOT** box.

Plot Scale
- Uncheck **FIT TO PAPER**. (If you do check this option, you will prevent your drawing from printing to scale.)
- Select **1:1** from the drop-down list.

Plot Style Table (Pen Assignments)
- Select **DDFD-FULL.CTB**.

Drawing Orientation
- Select **LANDSCAPE** or **PORTRAIT** to match the orientation of your sheet.

- **CLICK ONCE** the **OK** button to close the page setup dialog box.
- **CLICK ONCE** the **CLOSE** button to close the page setup manager dialog box.

- Finish setting up your viewport on page 96.

Page Setup Manager

Current layout: Sheet - 11x17

Page setups

Current page setup: <None>

Sheet - 11x17

[Set Current]
[New...]
[Modify...]
[Import...]

Selected page setup details

[Close]   [Help]

Page Setup - Sheet - 11x17

Page setup
Name: <None>

Printer / plotter
Name: None
Plotter: None

Paper size
Tabloid (11.00 x 17.00 Inches)

Plot area
What to plot:
Extents

Plot offset
X: [   ] ☑ Center the Plot
Y: [   ]

Plot scale
☐ Fit to paper
Scale: 1:1
1 inches
1 unit
☐ Scale lineweights

Plot style table
DDFD-Full.ctb
☐ Display plotsyles

Shaded viewport options

Plot options

Drawing Orientation
○ Portrait
◉ Landscape
☐ Plot upside-down

[OK]   [Close]   [Help]

18" × 24" – Setting Up an ARCH C-Sized Sheet

This sheet size is most commonly used for presentation drawings and construction documents. Most large format printers can print a 24" wide piece of paper and require a 0.75" margin.

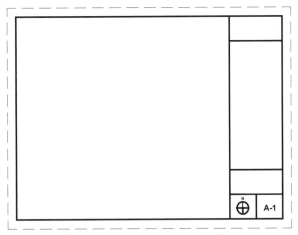

18" x 24" Construction Document Sheet with .75" margin

Construction Document Layout

· Set the current layer to **TB-BORDER**.
· Using the **RECTANGLE** command, draw a rectangle that is **24"** wide and **18"** tall.
· **OFFSET** the rectangle **0.75"** to the inside. This new rectangle represents the margins required by your printer. (With most printers, you cannot print to the edge of the paper.)
· **ERASE** the first rectangle. (You do not need this rectangle anymore.)
· Complete your title sheet so it matches the image to the left, using lines, circles, and text.

18" x 24" Presentation Drawing Sheet with .75" margin

Design Drawing Layout

· Set the current layer to **TB-BORDER**.
· Using the **RECTANGLE** command, draw a rectangle that is **24"** wide and **18"** tall.
· **OFFSET** the rectangle **0.75"** to the inside. This new rectangle represents the margins required by your printer. (With most printers, you cannot print to the edge of the paper.)
· **ERASE** the first rectangle. (You do not need this rectangle anymore.)
· Complete your title sheet so it matches the image to the left.

Set Up Your Page to Print

The **PAGE SETUP MANAGER** allows you to specify page layout and plotting device settings for each layout in your drawing. The page setup settings that you specify are stored within the layout, making it easy for you to print.

Page Setup Manager

Current layout: Sheet - 18x24

Page setups
Current page setup: <None>

Sheet - 18x24

Set Current
New...
Modify...
Import...

Selected page setup details

Close   Help

Page Setup - Sheet - 18x24

Page setup
Name: <None>

Printer / plotter
Name: None
Plotter: None

Paper size
ARCH C (18.00 x 24.00 Inches)

Plot area
What to plot:
Extents

Plot offset
X: ☑ Center the Plot
Y:

Plot scale
☐ Fit to paper
Scale: 1:1
1   inches =
1   unit
☐ Scale lineweights

Plot style table
DDFD-Full.ctb
☐ Display plotsyles

Shaded viewport options

Plot options

Drawing Orientation
○ Portrait
◉ Landscape
☐ Plot upside-down

OK   Close   Help

- From the **FILE** menu, select **PAGE SETUP MANAGER**.
- Click once on ***SHEET – 18×24*** (your sheet may have a different name).
- Click the **MODIFY** button.

Follow the steps below to complete the setup for your layout.

Printer/Plotter
- Select the printer you want use for this drawing. Printers installed on your computer are available for selection.

Paper Size
- This selection box will show paper sizes that are available for the printer you selected. Select **ARCH C**.

Plot Area
- This selection box allows you to customize what you want AutoCAD to print. Select **EXTENTS**.

Plot Offsets
- Place a checkmark in the **CENTER THE PLOT** box.

Plot Scale
- Uncheck **FIT TO PAPER**. (If you do check this option, you will prevent your drawing from printing to scale.)
- Select **1:1** from the drop-down list.

Plot Style Table (pen assignments)
- Select **DDFD-FULL.CTB**.

Drawing Orientation
- Select **LANDSCAPE** or **PORTRAIT** to match the orientation of your sheet.

- **CLICK ONCE** the **OK** button to close the page setup dialog box.
- **CLICK ONCE** the **CLOSE** button to close the page setup manager dialog box.

- Finish setting up your viewport on page 96.

24" × 36" – Setting Up an ARCH D-Sized Sheet
This sheet size is most commonly used for presentation drawings and construction documents. Most large format printers can print a 24" wide piece of paper and require a 0.75" margin.

**24" x 36" Construction Document Sheet
with .75" margin**

Construction Document Layout

· Set the current layer to **TB-BORDER.**
· Using the **RECTANGLE** command, draw a rectangle that is **36"** wide and **24"** tall.
· **OFFSET** the rectangle **0.75"** to the inside. This new rectangle represents the margins required by your printer. (With most printers, you cannot print to the edge of the paper.)
· **ERASE** the first rectangle. (You do not need this rectangle anymore.)
· Complete your title sheet so it matches the image to the left.

**24" x 36" Presentation Drawing Sheet
with .75" margin**

Design Drawing Layout

· Set the current layer to **TB-BORDER.**
· Using the **RECTANGLE** command, draw a rectangle that is **36"** wide and **24"** tall.
· **OFFSET** the rectangle **0.75"** to the inside. This new rectangle represents the margins required by your printer. (With most printers, you cannot print to the edge of the paper.)
· **ERASE** the first rectangle. (You do not need this rectangle anymore.)
· Complete your title sheet so it matches the image to the left.

Set Up Your Page to Print

The **PAGE SETUP MANAGER** allows you to specify page layout and plotting device settings for each layout in your drawing. The page setup settings that you specify are stored within the layout, making it easy for you to print.

- From the **FILE** menu, select **PAGE SETUP MANAGER**.
- Click once on ***SHEET – 24×36*** (your sheet may have a different name).
- Click the **MODIFY** button.

Follow the steps below to complete the setup for your layout.

Printer/Plotter
- Select the printer you want use for this drawing. Printers installed on your computer are available for selection.

Paper Size
- This selection box will show paper sizes that are available for the printer you selected. Select **ARCH D**.

Plot Area
- This selection box allows you to customize what you want AutoCAD to print. Select **EXTENTS**.

Plot Offsets
- Place a checkmark in the **CENTER THE PLOT** box.

Plot Scale
- Uncheck **FIT TO PAPER**. (If you do check this option, you will prevent your drawing from printing to scale.)
- Select **1:1** from the drop-down list.

Plot Style Table (pen assignments)
- Select **DDFD-FULL.CTB**.

Drawing Orientation
- Select **LANDSCAPE** or **PORTRAIT** to match the orientation of your sheet.

- **CLICK ONCE** the **OK** button to close the page setup dialog box.
- **CLICK ONCE** the **CLOSE** button to close the page setup manager dialog box.

- Finish setting up your viewport on page 96.

Page Setup Manager

Current layout: Sheet - 24x36

Page setups
Current page setup: <None>

Sheet - 24x36

Set Current
New...
Modify...
Import...

Selected page setup details

Close   Help

Page Setup - Sheet - 24x36

Page setup
Name: <None>

Printer / plotter
Name: None
Plotter: None

Paper size
ARCH D (24.00 x 36.00 Inches)

Plot area
What to plot:
Extents

Plot offset
X: ☑ Center the Plot
Y:

Plot scale
☐ Fit to paper
Scale: 1:1
1   inches =
1   unit
☐ Scale lineweights

Plot style table
DDFD-Full.ctb
☐ Display plotsyles

Shaded viewport options

Plot options

Drawing Orientation
○ Portrait
◉ Landscape
☐ Plot upside-down

OK   Close   Help

Creating a Viewport

The **VIEWPORT** command is very similar to the Rectangle command. AutoCAD will draw a viewport when you provide the location of two opposite corners. (You are drawing the diagonal of the rectangle.)

Viewports act like a window and allow you to see through your Layout View to Model Space.

· When you create your viewport, draw the viewport 1/8" inside the drawing portion of your title sheet. It is important that the viewport does not overlap any other lines in your drawing.

· Set the current layer to **TB-VIEWPORT**.

· Type the command **MVIEW** and press **ENTER**.
· **CLICK ONCE** in the drawing area where you want the lower left corner of your rectangle.
· Drag the AutoCAD cursor up and to the right. **CLICK ONCE** in the drawing area where you want the upper right corner of your rectangle.

· **ERASE** any construction lines used to create your viewport or title sheet.

Set the Scale for Your Viewport

The final step is to set the scale for the viewport you created.

- You can activate the viewport by **DOUBLE CLICKING** inside the viewport. You can de-activate the viewport by **DOUBLE CLICKING** outside the viewport.
- Clicking the Model/Paper button at the bottom of the AutoCAD screen will also activate and de-activate the viewport.

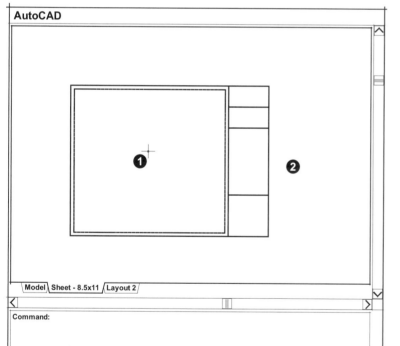

- With the mouse, **DOUBLE CLICK** inside the **VIEWPORT** created in the last step. This activates Model Space in your current layout.

If you have already started your drawing in Model Space, complete the step below. Otherwise skip to the next step.

- Type the command **ZOOM** and press **ENTER**. Type the letter **E** and press **ENTER**. (This fits your drawing in Model Space to the viewport.)

- Refer to page 62 to find the scale factor for your drawing scale. If you wanted to set the scale for this drawing at **1/8" = 1'-0"** you would see that the scale factor for **1/8" = 1'-0"** is **96**.

- Type the command **ZOOM** and press **ENTER**.

- Type **1/96XP** and press **ENTER**. You can change the **96** to match any scale factor listed at the beginning of this chapter.

Locking a Viewport

By locking the viewport, you will protect the scale of your drawing from accidentally changing as you work on your drawing.

```
AutoCAD

    Repeat...
    Recent Input...

    Maximize Viewport
    Viewport Clip
    Display Viewport Options

  ② Display Locked      ✓Yes ③
                         No
    Cut
    Copy

    Find
    Properties

  ①

Model \ Sheet - 8.5x11 / Layout 2 /

Command:
```

- With the mouse, **DOUBLE CLICK** outside the **VIEWPORT**. This de-activates the viewport.
- **CLICK ONCE** on the **VIEWPORT** to select it.
- **RIGHT CLICK** on the **VIEWPORT**. Go to **DISPLAY LOCKED** and select **YES**.

Drawing to Scale

Now that you have set up your layout, title block, and viewport, you can draw in either the **MODEL TAB** or the **LAYOUT TAB**.

- Drawing in the **LAYOUT TAB** (inside the activated viewport) is easier for some designers that are new to AutoCAD because it closely resembles drawing on a drafting table.

- **DOUBLE CLICK** inside the viewport and begin drawing your plan, section, or elevation.
- Draw lines at real world scale and AutoCAD will scale them to the scale of your viewport.

- Your drawing exists in both the **LAYOUT TAB** and the **MODEL TAB**. Remember the analogy of the window view back from the layout to the model tab.

Plot -

Page setup
Name: <None>

Printer / plotter
Name: Plotter
Plotter: None

Paper size
ARCH C (18.00 x 24.00 Inches)

Plot area
What to plot:
Extents

Plot offset
X: ☑ Center the Plot
Y:

Plot scale
☐ Fit to paper
Scale: 1:1
1 inches =
1 unit
☐ Scale lineweights

Plot style table
DDFD-FULL.ctb
☐ Display plotsyles

Shaded viewport options

Plot options

Drawing Orientation
○ Portrait
◉ Landscape
☐ Plot upside-down

Preview   OK   Close   Help

Plotting a Layout/Drawing

When you print a layout, AutoCAD will remember the settings in the Page Setup Manager.

· Type the command **PLOT** and press **ENTER**.

· Verify that the plotter and plot style are properly set.

· **CLICK** the **PREVIEW** button to see a preview of your print. While in the preview screen, you can zoom and pan around your drawing to check line weight and text fonts.

· If everything looks okay in the preview, press the **ESCAPE** key once and then click the **OK** button.

· If you need to make a change to the plot settings, press the **ESCAPE** key once, make the changes, and then **CLICK** the **PREVIEW** button.

· If you need to make a change to your drawing, press the **ESCAPE** key twice to exit the Plot dialog box. After you have made your adjustments, start over at the top of this page.

Learning Exercise

In this chapter exercise, you will set up a layout to print the floor plan you began in the previous chapter.

Open Your Drawing

· Open AutoCAD.
· Open the drawing you created in the previous chapter:
  DDFD-EAMES.DWG

Creating Your Layers

Create the following layers.

· **TB-VIEWPORT**   Color 31 NoPlot
· **TB-BORDER**   Color 1
· **TB-TEXT**   Color 5
· Set the current layer to **TB-BORDER.**

Drawing Your Layout

· Using the guides in this chapter, create an 18" × 24" landscape layout to match the drawing above.

· Save your drawing.

Creating Your Viewport

Using the guides in this chapter, set the scale of the viewport to **1/8"=1'-0"**.

· Set the current layer to **TB-VIEWPORT.**
· Using the **MVIEW** command, draw a viewport that matches the viewport in the drawing above (dashed line).

· Activate the viewport by double clicking inside the viewport.

· Use the zoom extents command to center your existing drawing in the viewport.

· Use the zoom command to scale your drawing to 1/8"=1'-0".

· De-activate the viewport by double clicking outside the viewport.

· Lock the viewport.

· Save your drawing.

· Congratulations, you have completed the learning exercise for this chapter.

CHAPTER 7
Text Styles and Sizes

Adding text to your drawing in AutoCAD is similar to using word processing software, with one exception: In a word processing program you control the height of text with the font size. Twelve-point Arial text will always print the same height—regardless of the word processing software and regardless of the printer.

In AutoCAD, determining the size of the text is slightly more complicated. Text height is determined by the desired printed text height and the scale of your drawing. For example, if you want your text to print 1/8" tall and your drawing is scaled at 1/16" = 1'-0" then you will need to set the text height (in AutoCAD) to 2'-0".

Sound confusing? It is.
That is why this chapter includes a few key charts to help you master adding text to your AutoCAD drawings.

Drawing Scale and Text Size

The text on your digital drawings should be sized appropriately. Understanding the relationship between drawing scale and text size in AutoCAD requires observation of drawings at different scales with similar text.

PLAN - 1/4"=1'-0"

- If you are working on a presentation drawing, the text must be legible from a few feet away.
- If you are working on construction drawings, the text must be legible from a few inches away.
- In general, text should be added to your drawing in **MODEL SPACE**.

Text Height 1/4" = 1'-0"

- The plan to the left is printed at **1/4"=1'-0"**.
- The text label living room measures 1/8" tall with a ruler (on the right).
- The text label living room measures 6" tall with an architectural scale (on the left).

PLAN - 1/8"=1'-0"

Text Height 1/8" = 1'-0"

- The plan to the left is printed at **1/8"=1'-0"**.
- The text label living room measures 1/8" tall with a ruler (on the right).
- The text label living room measures 12" tall with an architectural scale (on the left).

- As the drawing scale gets smaller, the scaled text height gets taller.

Calculating Text Height

- When you add text to your drawings, you will draw it at an enlarged size so that it will print consistently through your presentation or drawing set.
- Appropriate text height can be easily calculated. Multiply the desired printed text height (1/8") by the scale factor for the current drawing scale (48, 96, 192, and so on) to get the appropriate text height.
1/8" × 96 = 12"

		Printed Text Height		
Drawing Scale	Scale Factor	1/4"	1/8"	3/32"
3"=1'-0"	4	1"	1/2"	3/8"
1 1/2"=1'-0"	8	2"	1"	3/4"
1"=1'-0"	12	3"	1-1/2"	1-1/8"
3/4"=1'-0"	16	4"	2"	1-1/2"
1/2"=1'-0"	24	6"	3"	2-1/4"
3/8"=1'-0"	32	8"	4"	3"
1/4"=1'-0"	48	12"	6"	4-1/2"
3/16"=1'-0"	64	1'-4"	8"	6"
1/8"=1'-0"	96	2'-0"	12"	9"
3/32"=1'-0"	128	2'-8"	1'-4"	12"
1/16"=1'-0"	192	4'-0"	2'-0"	1'-6"
1/32=1'-0"	384	8'-0"	4'-0"	3'-0"

- You can use the chart to the left to determine the appropriate text height for imperial scaled drawings.

- 1/4" tall text is commonly found in title blocks.
- 1/8" tall text is appropriate for notes in most design drawings.
- 3/32" tall text is most commonly found in construction documents.

		Printed Text Height		
Drawing Scale	Scale Factor	1/4"	1/8"	3/32"
1:10	10	2.5	1.25	0.9375
1:20	20	5.0	2.50	1.8750
1:50	50	12.5	6.25	4.6875
1:100	100	25.0	12.50	9.3750

- You can use the chart to the left to determine the appropriate text height for metric scaled drawings.

Text Styles

Text styles allow you to define different text font preferences in your AutoCAD drawing. You will need to set up at least one text style before you add text to you drawing.

- There are two types of fonts available in AutoCAD: AutoCAD fonts and TrueType fonts.

AutoCAD Fonts

- AutoCAD fonts have an .shx extension.
- The weight of an AutoCAD font is determined by the color of its layer. This behavior is the same as the relationship between line color and line weight.

AUTOCAD FONTS			
TXT.SHX	ABCDEFGHIJKLMNOPQRSTUVWXYZ	1234567890	COLOR 7
SIMPLEX.TXT	ABCDEFGHIJKLMNOPQRSTUVWXYZ	1234567890	
TXT.SHX	ABCDEFGHIJKLMNOPQRSTUVWXYZ	1234567890	COLOR 5
SIMPLEX.TXT	ABCDEFGHIJKLMNOPQRSTUVWXYZ	1234567890	

TRUE TYPE FONTS		
ARIAL	ABCDEFGHIJKLMNOPQRSTUVWXYZ	1234567890
ARIAL (BOLD)	**ABCDEFGHIJKLMNOPQRSTUVWXYZ**	**1234567890**
CITY BLUEPRINT	ABCDEFGHIJKLMNOPQRSTUVWXYZ	1234567890
COUNTRY BLUEPRINT	ABCDEFGHIJKLMNOPQRSTUVWXYZ	1234567890

TrueType Fonts

- TrueType fonts have a TT icon and are available in all Windows programs, including Word Perfect and Microsoft Word.
- The weight of a TrueType font is determined by the font style setting (bold, italic, and so on).
- Some fonts, like city blueprint and country blueprint, cannot print bold in AutoCAD and are difficult to read in presentations and construction drawings.

Adding a Text Style

The Text Style dialog box allows you to create and modify text styles in the current drawing. Text styles are stored separately in each Auto-CAD drawing.

Text Style ✕

Style Name
Arial ▾ [New] [Rename] [Delete]   [Apply]   [Close]   [Help]

Font

| Font Name | Font Style | Height |
| Arial ▾ | Bold ▾ | 0" |

☐ Use Big Font

Effects
☐ Upside down Width Factor [1.000]
☐ Backwards
☐ Vertical Oblique Angle [0]

- Type the command **STYLE** and press **ENTER**.
- **CLICK ONCE** the **NEW** button.
- Type the style name **ARIAL** and click the **OK** button.
- From the **FONT NAME** drop-down list, select **ARIAL**.
- From the **FONT STYLE** drop-down list, select **REGULAR**.
- Set the **HEIGHT** to **0'-0"**. You will set the height for the text when you add it to your drawing.
- **CLICK ONCE** the **CLOSE** button.

Adding Text

The **TEXT** command allows you to add text to your drawing. We will add a line of text to a drawing scaled at 1/8" = 1'-0".

AutoCAD

this is sample text

Command:

- Type the command **TEXT** and press **ENTER**.
- **CLICK ONCE** in AutoCAD where you want to start your text. (You can move the text location in your drawing after you complete the **TEXT** command.)
- AutoCAD prompts you for the text height. Refer to the chart at the beginning of this chapter to see that the text height for a 1/8" = 1'-0" drawing should be 12". Type **12** and press **ENTER**.
- AutoCAD prompts you for the text rotation. Type **0** and press **ENTER**.
- Type **THIS IS SAMPLE TEXT** and press **ENTER**.
- Press **ENTER** one more time to finish the Text command.

Adding Multiline Text

The **MTEXT** command allows you to add multiline text to your drawing. We will add text to a
drawing scaled at 1/8" = 1'-0".

· Type the command **MTEXT** and press **ENTER**.

· **CLICK ONCE** in AutoCAD where you want to
start your text. (You can move the text location in your drawing after you complete the
MTEXT command.)

· **CLICK ONCE** in AutoCAD where you want the
lower right corner of your text box. This text
box will determine the width and line wrap
for the text in your drawing. You can modify
the size of this box after you have finished
the **MTEXT** command.

· The Text Formatting dialog box prompts you
for the text style and text height.
Select **ARIAL** from the Text Style drop-down
list. Refer to the chart on the previous page
to see that the text height for a 1/8" = 1'-0"
drawing should be 12".
Type **12** and press **ENTER**.

· In the text box, type **THIS IS SAMPLE MULTILINE
TEXT** and click the **OK** button.

Text Formatting

| arial | Ti Arial | 12.000 | B | I | U | OK |

this is sample
multiline text

Editing Text

The **DDEDIT** command allows you to edit text and multiline text in your drawing.

- Type the command **DDEDIT** and press **ENTER**.
- **CLICK ONCE** on the text that you want to edit.
- If you are editing **SINGLE LINE TEXT**, complete your text edits and press **ENTER**.
- If you are editing **MULTILINE TEXT**, complete your text edit and click the **OK** button.
- Press **ENTER** one more time to end the **DDEDIT** command.

AutoCAD

General	≫
Color	ByLayer
Layer	a-wall
Linetype	ByLayer
Linetype scale	1.00
Plot style	ByColor
Thickness	0"

Text	≫
Contents	1ST FLOO
Style	Standard
Justify	Left
Height	1/8"
Rotation	0
Width Factor	1.0000
Obliquing	0

Geometry	≫

PROPERTIES

1ST FLOOR

Command:

Editing Text Height

- You can change the height of text in your drawing with the Properties Palette.
- To open the Properties Palette, type **CH** and press **ENTER**.
- **CLICK ONCE** on the text that you want to modify.
- The Text section of the palette displays the text's Style, Justification, Height, Rotation, and Width Factor.
- Changing the value of the height variable will change the height of the selected text.
- Press the **ESCAPE** key twice to deselect the text and end the text modification.

UTILITY ROOM

LIVING ROOM

KITCHEN

DINING ROOM

Learning Exercise

In this chapter exercise, you will add the text labels to the floor plan you began in the previous chapters.

Open Your Drawing

· Open AutoCAD.
· Open the drawing you created in the previous chapter:
  DDFD-EAMES.DWG

Creating Your Layers

Create the following layers:

· **A-TEXT**   Color 5
· Set the current layer to **A-TEXT.**

Adding a Text Style

· Open the Text Style manager and set the font for the standard text style to **ARIAL BOLD**.

Adding Text Labels to Your Plan

· Using the **TEXT** command, add the appropriate labels to your drawing to match the drawing above.

· Refer to the charts at the beginning of this chapter to determine to appropriate text height (the text should print 1/8" tall).

· Save your drawing.

DARK ROOM

COURTYARD

STUDIO

FIRST FLOOR PLAN
EAMES HOUSE - 1949

N

Adding Text to Your Layout

· Set the current layer to **TB-TEXT.**

· Using the **TEXT** command, add the appropriate labels to your layout/ title block to match the drawing to the left.

· The title text should be 1/4" tall. The other text should be 1/8" tall.

· Save your drawing.

· Congratulations, you have completed the learning exercise for this chapter.

CHAPTER 8

Hatches and Dashed Lines

The topics discussed in this chapter should be familiar to you from your experience drafting by hand. Hatches are used to indicate material in plan, elevation, section, or detail. Dashed lines are used to indicate an object position relative to the cutting plane. Dashed lines can also be used to indicate special wall assemblies (e.g., fire rated walls).

These two graphic conventions take a considerable amount of time and attention in manual drawing. AutoCAD simplifies the process of adding each to your design drawings.

Drawing Hatch Patterns

Hatch patterns are used in design drawings as graphic shorthand to symbolize specific materials in your drawing. AutoCAD contains a series of predefined hatches that match acceptable industry standards.

You should consider the following when adding hatch patterns to your drawings:

· The scale of your drawing or detail may inform the scale of the hatch pattern.
· Materials are identified with different hatch patters in plan, section, and elevation.
· Hatches are an additional layer of information you communicate in design drawings. Make sure your hatches do not visually overpower your drawing.
· The **BHATCH** command fills a predrawn area in your drawing with a hatch pattern. If the lines defining the edge of the material are not connected at all endpoints, AutoCAD will not be able to properly identify your desired fill area.

Adding Hatch Patterns

In the example to the left, we will fill the floor slab in the detail with a concrete hatch.

Create the following layers. You can open the layer properties manager by typing the command **LAYER** and pressing **ENTER**.
· **A-HATCH** Color 8
· Set the current layer to **A-HATCH**.

· Type the command **BHATCH** and press **ENTER** to open the Hatch and Gradient dialog box.
· **CLICK ONCE** the button to the right of the current pattern. This will open the Hatch Pattern Palette.

Hatch Pattern Palette

| ANSI | ISO | Other Predefined | Custom |

AR-B88   AR-BRELM   AR-BRSTD   AR-CONC

OK   Close   Help

CLICK ONCE the **OTHER PREDEFINED** tab at the top of the Hatch Pattern Palette.

CLICK ONCE the **AR-CONC** hatch pattern and click the **OK** button.

Hatch and Gradient

Hatch | Gradient

Type and pattern

Type: Predefined

Pattern: AR-CONC   ...

Swatch:

Angle and scale

Angle: Scale:

0   0.25

Hatch origin

◉ Use current origin
○ Specified origin

Boundaries

+   Add: Pick points

+   Add: Select objects

Options

☑ Associative

☐ Create separate hatches

Draw order:

Send behind boundary

Preview   OK   Close   Help

CLICK ONCE the **ADD: PICK POINTS** button at the top of the Hatch Pattern Palette.

· When you click this button, the Boundary Hatch dialog box will disappear and Auto-CAD will prompt you to pick an internal point. **CLICK ONCE** anywhere inside the area you want to fill with the Concrete hatch.

· When you are through selecting areas to fill, press **ENTER**.

· Change the scale value to **0.25**.

CLICK ONCE the **PREVIEW** button to see a pre-view of your hatch.

· If you are satisfied with the hatch preview, press **ENTER** to end the **BHATCH** command.

· If you are not satisfied with the hatch preview, press **ESC** to go back to the Hatch and Gradient dialog box. Make any required changes and click the **PREVIEW** button to review your hatch.

HATCH PATTERN

SECTIONS/DETAILS
1 1/2" = 1'-0"

AR-SAND

TWO LAYERS OF
5/8" GWB

AR-SAND
SCALE: .25

AR-CONC

6" CONC SLAB

AR-CONC
SCALE: 0.25

ANSI31

CLAY BRICK &
MORTAR

ANSI31
SCALE: 3.0

ANSI32

+ =

PLYWOOD
COMBINE ANSI32 WITH
VERTICAL LINES
ANSI32
SCALE: 4.0

MULTIPLE ARCS

HARDWOOD
(HEAVY TIMBER)

MULTIPLE ARCS
(NO HATCH)

Section/Detail Hatch Patterns
· The following hatch patterns are included with AutoCAD and appropriate for objects drawn in section.
· An appropriate hatch scale is listed for different drawing scales. You may modify these scales to your preference.

Drywall – In Detail
· AR-SAND
· Hatch Scale: 0.3–0.5
  for drawings larger than 1-1/2" = 1'-0"

Concrete – In Detail
· AR-CONC
· Hatch Scale: 0.50–1.0

Brick – In Detail
· ANSI31
· Hatch Scale: 5.0
  for drawings larger than 1-1/2" = 1'-0"

Plywood – In Detail
· The plywood section hatch is created by combining lines and the ANSI32 hatch pattern.
· The lines represent the plies in the wood and run the length of the wood in section.

Hardwood – In Detail
· The hardwood section hatch is created by copying multiple circles and trimming the portion of the circle that exists outside the hardwood.

HATCH PATTERN

ELEVATION/PLAN
1/4" = 1'-0"

AR-SAND

PLASTER WALL

AR-SAND
SCALE: 12

AR-SAND

CONCRETE FLOOR

AR-SAND
SCALE: 12

AR-BRSTD

BRICK WALL

AR-BRSTD
SCALE: 1.0

GRAVEL

FIELDSTONE FLOOR

GRAVEL
SCALE: 24

ANSI37

8" TILE FLOOR
ANSI37
SCALE: 64/ROTATION:45

12" TILE FLOOR
ANSI37
SCALE: 96/ROTATION:45

Elevation/Plan Hatch Patterns

· The following hatch patterns are included with AutoCAD and appropriate for objects drawn in plan or elevation.
· An appropriate hatch scale is listed for different drawing scales. You may modify these scales to your preference.

Plaster – Elevation/Plan
· AR-SAND
· Hatch Scale: 3.0–12.0
  for 1/16" = 1'-0" to 1/4" = 1'-0"

Concrete – Elevation/Plan
· AR-SAND
· Hatch Scale: 3.0–12.0
  for 1/16" = 1'-0" to 1/4" = 1'-0"

Brick – Elevation
· AR-BRSTD
· Hatch Scale: 1.0

Field Stone – Plan
· GRAVEL
· Hatch Scale: 24.0

8" Tile – Plan
· ANSI37
· Hatch Scale: 64.0/Rotation: 45
12" Tile – Plan
· ANSI37
· Hatch Scale: 96.0/Rotation: 45

Line Type

Understanding how to use clear and legible line types will better communicate your design drawings than any combination of AutoCAD commands. You most likely have been introduced to these concepts in a manual drafting studio, conceptual drawing studio, or design studio.

- Drawing dashed lines by hand can be a time consuming process.
- In AutoCAD, you adjust line type by selecting different line types for different kinds of lines.

Industry Standard Line Types

- The following line types are included with AutoCAD.

HIDDEN2 (Color 5) _ _ _ _ _ _ _ _ _ _ _ _ _ _ _ _ _

- Hidden Line – Used in drawing to indicate objects that are above the cutting plane or hidden beyond objects in the current view.

CENTER2 (Color 5) ___ _ ___ _ ___ _ ___

- Center Line – Used in drawings to indicate the center of an object. It is usually used in combination with dimensions.

PHANTOM2 (Color 5) _ _ ___ _ _ ___ _ _ _

- Property Line – The **PHANTOM2** line type is used to indicate property lines in site plans.

- Fire Rating – A variation of the **CENTER2** and **DIVIDE2** line types can be used to indicate wall fire ratings in floor plans. Draw an additional polyline in the center of the indicated wall. Adjust the thickness of the polyline so the line will clearly communicate your desired wall ratings.

CENTER2 (Color 5) ▬ ▪ ▬ ▪ ▬ ▪ ▬

- **CENTER2** can be used for one-hour rated wall assemblies.

DIVIDE2 (Color 5) ▪ ▮ ▬ ▮ ▬ ▮ ▬ ▮ ▬

- **DIVIDE2** can be used for two-hour rated wall assemblies.

Layer Properties Manager

Name	On	Freeze	Lock	Color	Linetype
0				white	Continuous
A-WALL				red	Continuous
A-WALL-ABOV				blue	Hidden2
A-DOOR				green	Continuous

Current Layer: 0

Select Linetype

Loaded Linetypes

Linetype	Appearance
Continuous	
CENTER2	
HIDDEN2	

OK Cancel Load Help

Load or Reload Linetypes

File...

Available Linetypes

Linetype	Appearance
CENTER	
CENTER2	
CENTER2X	

OK Cancel Help

Adding Line Types to Your Drawing

- Open the Layer Manager. (Type the command **LAYER** and press **ENTER**.)
- Create a new layer for each unique line type (i.e., A-Wall-Abov).
- **CLICK ONCE** the line type description for the layer you want to modify. This will open the Select Linetype dialog box.
- Select the linetype you want to assign to your new layer or **CLICK ONCE** the **LOAD** button to add additional linetypes to your drawing.
- In the Load or Reload Linetypes dialog box, scroll down the list of available linetypes. **CLICK ONCE** on the appropriate linetype and click the **OK** button to load the linetype into your drawing.
- In the Select Linetypes dialog box, **CLICK ONCE** on the linetype and click the **OK** button to set this as the linetype for your new layer.

Drawing Scale	Scale Factor	LTScale
3"=1'-0"	4	2
1 1/2"=1'-0"	8	4
1"=1'-0"	12	6
3/4"=1'-0"	16	8
1/2"=1'-0"	24	12
3/8"=1'-0"	32	16
1/4"=1'-0"	48	24
3/16"=1'-0"	64	32
1/8"=1'-0"	96	48
3/32"=1'-0"	128	64
1/16"=1'-0"	192	96
1/32=1'-0"	384	192

Line-Type Scale

The **LTSCALE** setting helps AutoCAD adjust the size of the dashes to match your drawing scale. You only need to adjust this setting once per drawing. In general, the **LTSCALE** is set to 1/2 of the scale factor for your drawing.

Setting the Ltscale

- Type the command **LTSCALE** and press **ENTER**.
- Type the appropriate **LTSCALE** from the chart to the left and press **ENTER**.
- In each of your layouts, type **PSLTSCALE** and press **ENTER**. Type **0** and press **ENTER**.

Learning Exercise

In this chapter exercise, you will add visual hierarchy to the wall in your plan through poché. You will use the Hatch command to poché the walls.

Open Your Drawing

· Open AutoCAD.
· Open the drawing you created in the previous chapter:
  DDFD-EAMES.DWG

Creating Your Layers

Create the following layers:

· **A-WALL-HATCH**   Color 9
· Set the current layer to **A-WALL-HATCH.**

Hatching Your Walls

· Using the Hatch command, poché the walls (indicated above) with pattern ANSI31 and hatch scale 10.

· Save your drawing.

DARK ROOM

COURTYARD

STUDIO

UTILITY ROOM

LIVING ROOM

KITCHEN

DINING ROOM

Learning Exercise

In this chapter exercise, you will use dashed and continuous lines to add the stairs to your floor plan.

Open Your Drawing

· Open AutoCAD.
· Open the drawing you created in the previous chapter:
  DDFD-EAMES.DWG

Creating Your Layers

Create the following layers:

· **A-FLOR-ABOV**   Color 6   HIDDEN2
· **A-FLOR-STAIR**   Color 7   Continuous
· Set the current layer to **A-FLOR-ABOV.**

Adding Stairs

· Using the line command and the offset command, draw the stair in the workshop.
· Using the circle command and the offset command, draw the circular stair in the main residence.

· Save your drawing.

Congratulations, you have completed the learning exercise for this chapter.

DARK ROOM

COURTYARD

STUDIO

9'-2"

10'

3'-3"

3'-0"

ADVANCED DRAWING TOOLS

CHAPTER 9
Stencils and Blocks

One advantage to drawing in AutoCAD is the ability to quickly move drawing symbols (like toilets, doors, and furniture) between drawings. It may take you 10 minutes to draw a chaise lounge in AutoCAD, but you can insert that chair as a block into any other AutoCAD drawing in less than a minute.

Consider the following questions as you work through this chapter:

· How are AutoCAD blocks similar to drawing stencils?
· How do you move AutoCAD blocks between drawings?

Drawing with Stencils

A stencil helps you quickly and accurately add symbols like toilets, doors, and sinks to your drawing. The AutoCAD equivalent to the drawing stencil is the **block** command.

Stencils

· You can purchase stencils with various themes, including kitchen design and bathroom design.
· Stencils are scale specific, so you need different stencils for 1/8" = 1'-0" and 1/4" = 1'-0".

Blocks

· You can make a custom block to use as a symbol in your drawing or you can insert predefined blocks into your drawings.
· Blocks are always drawn at full scale (like everything else in AutoCAD), so a single toilet block can be used in various scaled drawings.
· Blocks can be shared among AutoCAD drawings.
· Blocks group lines together into a single object.

· The drawings in the AutoCAD window to the left are all blocks.

Creating a Block

The following steps will guide you through the process of creating a custom block. In this example, we will make a block of a toilet.

· **Step 1:** Move all the lines you are using to create your block onto Layer 0.

· **Step 2:** Type the command **BLOCK** and press **ENTER**. This will open the Block Definition dialog box.

· **Step 3:** Type the name for your block. Block names can have up to 255 characters. The block name will help you identify this block and other blocks in your drawing. Type the name **TOILET**.

Step 4: The Objects portion of the Block Definition dialog box allows you to select the lines that you want to add to your block.
· **CLICK ONCE** on the **CONVERT TO BLOCK BUTTON**.

· **CLICK ONCE** on the **SELECT OBJECTS BUTTON**.
· The Block Definition dialog box will disappear, allowing you to select the lines for your block. Draw a **WINDOW SELECTION** around the lines that make the toilet.
· Press **ENTER** when you have finished selecting objects for your block.

Step 5: The Base Point portion of the Block Definition dialog box allows you to select the base point or reference point for your block. This point will be the reference point when you insert additional copies of this block.
· **CLICK ONCE** on the **PICK POINT BUTTON**.
· The Block Definition dialog box will disappear, allowing you to select the base point for your block. Using object snaps, **CLICK ONCE** on the **MIDPOINT** of the toilet tank.

Step 6: CLICK ONCE on the **OK** button to complete your block.

Inserting Blocks into Your Drawing

The following steps will guide you through the process of adding or inserting a block into your drawing. In this example, we insert the toilet block created in the previous section.

- **Step 1:** Type the command **INSERT** and press **ENTER**. This will open the Insert dialog box.

- **Step 2:** The Name drop-down menu lists all the blocks that are currently in your drawing. Select the **TOILET** block from this list.

- **Step 3:** In the Insertion Point portion of the dialog box, **CHECK** the **SPECIFY ON-SCREEN** option.
- In the Scale portion of the dialog box, **UNCHECK** the **SPECIFY ON-SCREEN** option and set the scale values to **1.00**.
- In the Rotation portion of the dialog box, **UNCHECK** the **SPECIFY ON-SCREEN** option and set the rotation value to **0**.

- **Step 4: CLICK ONCE** on the **OK** button to complete your block.

- **Step 5:** After you click the OK button, the Insert dialog box will disappear. The AutoCAD cursor will have the toilet block attached to it.
- **CLICK ONCE** where you want to insert the toilet block. You can modify the position of any block after it is inserted into your drawing.

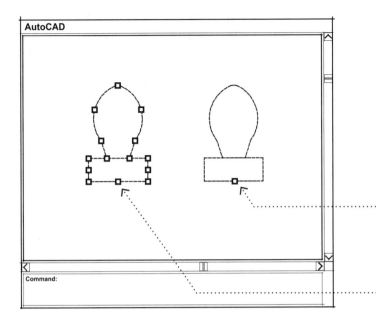

Exploding Blocks

The **EXPLODE** command will convert a block back into its original objects. Once you explode a block, you can no longer make global changes to the block.

· Type the command **EXPLODE** and press **ENTER**.
· **CLICK ONCE** on the block in your drawing.
· Press **ENTER**.

· In the example, the toilet on the right is a block. When you select a block, you will see one grip (which is located at the block's base point).

· In the example, the toilet on the left is an exploded block. When you select an exploded block, you will see grips for each AutoCAD object.

Exporting Blocks

The **WBLOCK** command (short for Write Block) will export any block in your drawing so you can use it in other AutoCAD drawings.

· Type the command **WBLOCK** and press **ENTER**.
· Select **BLOCK** as your source.
· The Block drop-down menu lists all the blocks that are currently in your drawing. Select the **TOILET** block from this list.
· In the Destination portion of the Write Block dialog box, select the place on your computer where you want to save your exported block.
· **CLICK ONCE** on the **OK** button to complete your block export.

· You can create a folder on your computer where you keep all of your blocks for future drawings.

Edit Block Definitions

Block to create or edit:

Toilet

Preview

Description

| OK | Cancel | Help |

Editing Blocks

One advantage of using blocks in AutoCAD is the ability to make global changes. For example, if you modify a chair block, every version of that block will automatically update in the current drawing.

· Type the command **BEDIT** (short for block edit) and press **ENTER**. This will open the Edit Block Definition dialog box.
· Select the block that you want to edit and click **OK**.
· AutoCAD will open the block in edit mode. You can add, subtract, or modify any line within the block.
· When you have finished editing the block, type the command **BCLOSE** and press **ENTER**.

· AutoCAD will prompt you to save changes to the current block. If you click **YES**, all versions of the block will be updated in the current drawing. If you click **NO**, nothing will be updated and all changes will be lost.

Learning Exercise

In this exercise, you will create a door block and insert it into your floor plan.

Open Your Drawing

· Open AutoCAD.
· Open the drawing you created in the previous chapter: **DDFD-EAMES.DWG**

Creating Your Layers

Create the following layers:

· **A-DOOR**   Color 7
· Set the current layer to **0**.

Drawing the Door

· Using the line command and the circle command, draw a door with the dimensions above.
· Using the block command, create a block of the door using the insertion point indicated above. Name the block **DOOR**.
  NOTE: Before you create your block, make sure the lines are all on Layer **0** and have their color set to **BYLAYER**.

· Save your drawing.

DARK ROOM

COURTYARD

STUDIO

Inserting the Door

· Set the current layer to **A-DOOR.**
· Using the insert command, insert the three doors indicated in the plan above. You can insert one door and copy it to each location or insert the door three separate times.

· Save your drawing.

Congratulations, you have completed the learning exercise for this chapter.

CHAPTER 10
Advanced Editing Tools

At this point in your AutoCAD education, you know most of the commands and concepts required to create a presentation-quality design drawing. This chapter discusses several different editing tools that will help you complete common editing tasks in a shorter period of time.

Consider the following questions as you work through this chapter:
- How can the concepts and commands in this chapter help me draw more efficiently?
- Many of the commands in this chapter are a combination of multiple commands you already know. What commands would you combine to achieve the same result as the commands discussed in this chapter?

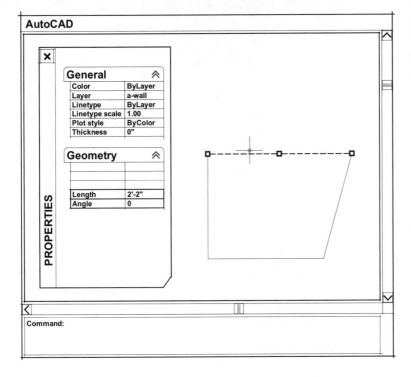

Properties Palette

The **PROPERTIES PALETTE** displays and controls the properties of objects in your drawing.

- Properties displayed include the object's Layer, Color, and Rotation.
- When more than one object is selected, the Properties palette displays only the common properties of the selected objects.
- To open the **PROPERTIES PALETTE**, type **CH** and press **ENTER**.

Line Properties

When you select a line in your drawing, the **PROPERTIES PALETTE** will display information about the line selected.

- The General section in the palette displays the line's Color, Layer, Linetype, Linetype Scale, and Thickness.
- The Layer and Linetype should be set to **BYLAYER**. The Linetype Scale should be set to **1.0**.
- The Geometry section displays the length and angle of the line. This is one way to verify the length of a line in your drawing.

Text Properties

When you select text in your drawing, the **PROPERTIES PALETTE** will display information about the text selected.

- The General section in the palette displays the line's Color, Layer, Linetype, Linetype Scale, and Thickness.
- The Text section of the palette displays the text's Style, Justification, Height, Rotation, and Width Factor.
- This is an easy and common method to adjust text justification, text height, and text rotation.

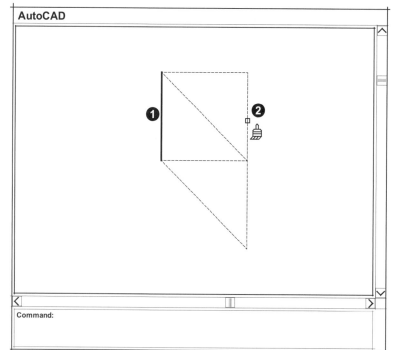

Match Properties

The Match Properties command allows you to copy the properties of one object to other objects in your drawing.

- Matchprop is a quick way to move a large number of lines to a specific layer.
- Matchprop will copy the following properties for lines, circles, and arcs: Color, Layer, Linetype, Linetype Scale, and Thickness.
- Matchprop will copy the following properties for text: Color, Layer, Linetype, Linetype Scale, Thickness, Style, Justification, Height, Rotation, and Width Factor.

- Type the command **MATCHPROP** and press **ENTER**.
- **Step 1**: **CLICK ONCE** on the object whose properties you want to copy.
- **Step 2**: **CLICK ONCE** on the destination objects (the objects to which you want to copy the properties). You can select the destination objects one at a time or with the Crossing window selection.
- Press **ENTER** on the keyboard to end the **MATCHPROP** command.

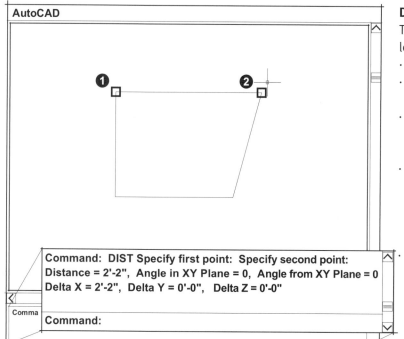

Distance

The Distance command allows you to verify the length of a line or space within your drawing.

- Type the command **DI** and press **ENTER**.
- **Step 1**: Using the mouse, **OBJECT SNAP** on the first point of your distance inquiry.
- **Step 2**: Using the mouse, **OBJECT SNAP** on the second point of your distance inquiry.

- The distance is reported in the command prompt. Information displayed includes the **DISTANCE**, the angle of the line, the horizontal distance (**DELTA X**), and the vertical distance (**DELTA Y**).
- A horizontal line will have a matching **DISTANCE** and horizontal distance (**DELTA X**). A vertical line will have a matching **DISTANCE** and vertical distance (**DELTA Y**).

Command: DIST Specify first point: Specify second point:
Distance = 2'-2", Angle in XY Plane = 0, Angle from XY Plane = 0
Delta X = 2'-2", Delta Y = 0'-0", Delta Z = 0'-0"

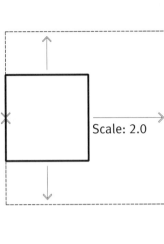

Scale: 2.0

Scale: 2.0

Base Point

Scale: 0.5

Scale: 0.75

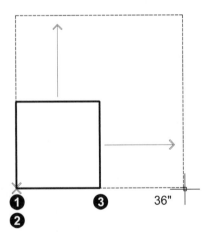

①
②   **③**   36"

Scale

The Scale command allows you to adjust the size of an object or group of objects in your drawing.

- Type the command **SCALE** and press **ENTER**.
- Using the mouse, select the objects you want to scale. Press **ENTER** when you have finished selecting objects.
- Using the mouse, **SELECT THE BASE POINT** for your scale. The base point is the point from which your objects will grow or shrink.
- Type the **SCALE FACTOR** and press **ENTER**. To make something twice its original size, scale it by **2**. To make something half its original size, scale it by **0.5**.

Scale Reference

The Scale Reference command allows you to adjust the size of an object or group of objects in your drawing based on your desired length for a part of the selected object.

- There are times when you will receive a floor plan that is not drawn at real world scale. Using Scale Reference, you can adjust the scale of an unscaled floor plan so the door openings are 36".

- Type the command **SCALE** and press **ENTER**.
- **Step 1**: Using the mouse, select the objects you want to scale. In this example, you want to select the entire plan. Type **ALL** and press **ENTER**. Press **ENTER** one more time.
- Using the mouse, **SELECT THE BASE POINT** for your scale. The base point is the point from which your objects will grow or shrink.
- Type the letter **R** and press **ENTER**.
- **Steps 2 and 3**: Define the reference length by object snapping to either end of the door-jamb.
- Type the desired length (**36"**) and press **ENTER**.

AutoCAD

Pass 2 892   objects audited
Pass 3 1012   objects audited
Total errors found 0 fixed 0

Comma

Command:

Audit

The Audit command looks through your Auto-CAD file for errors or problems. The command will take longer to complete on larger files and slower computers.

· Run the Audit command when you first open a drawing received from a consultant or from another designer.
· You can run the Audit command on your own drawings after a file crash.

· Type the command **AUDIT** and press **ENTER**.
· AutoCAD prompts you to fix errors detected. Type the letter **Y** and press **ENTER**.
· You have successfully audited your drawing.

Purge ☒

- ⦿ **View items you can purge**
- ○ **View items you cannot purge**

Items not used in drawing

> **All Items**
>> **Blocks**
>> **Dimension styles**
>> **Layers**
>> **Linetypes**

- ☐ **Confirm each item to be purged**
- ☑ **Purge nested items**

| Purge | Purge All | Close | Help |

Purge

The Purge command will clean your drawing of items that are taking up space but are no longer being used in your drawing. These items can include blocks, layers, text styles, and dimension styles.

· Type the command **PURGE** and press **ENTER**. AutoCAD will open the Purge dialog box.
· To purge individual items, select them from the "Items not used in drawing" area and **CLICK** the **PURGE** button.
· To purge all unused items in your drawing, place a checkmark in the "Purge nested items" option and **CLICK** the **PURGE ALL** button.
· Click the **CLOSE** button and **SAVE** your drawing.

AutoCAD Express Tools

The AutoCAD Express Tools are a collection of program enhancements that simplify many commands within AutoCAD. When installed, they are integrated into the AutoCAD menus and toolbars. The following pages describe several Express Tools that are commonly used when drawing in AutoCAD.

· Express Tools enhance a wide range of AutoCAD functions, including layer management, dimensioning, drawing, object selection, and object modification.

· Express Tools are included with versions of AutoCAD released after 2004 but may need to be installed separately from AutoCAD. (Check your AutoCAD CD for an Express folder.)

· Express Tools Vols. 1–9, which can be purchased from the AutoCAD store, work with all AutoCAD 2002–, 2000i–, and 2000–based products.

· Express Tools are not compatible with AutoCAD LT.

Flatten (Express Tool)

Although AutoCAD allows you to draw in three dimensions, 99 percent of all design drawings created in AutoCAD are two-dimensional.

· The **FLATTEN** command will adjust the **Z COORDINATE** of all objects in your drawing to **0** . This can be an important first step when you receive drawings from consultants or other designers.

· Type the command **FLATTEN** and press **ENTER**.
· Using the mouse, select the objects you want to flatten. In most cases, you want to flatten the entire drawing. Type **ALL** and press **ENTER**. Press **ENTER** one more time.
· AutoCAD prompts you to remove hidden lines. Type the letter **Y** and press **ENTER**.
· You have successfully flattened all the objects in your drawing.

OVERKILL

Object comparison settings

☐ Ignore LAYERS   Numeric Fuzz   `0.00`
☐ Ignore LINETYPE
☐ Ignore COLOR
☐ Ignore LINEWEIGHT
☐ Ignore PLOTSTYLE

Lines, Arcs and Plines

☑ PLINES - Optimize segments within plines
☑ OVERLAP - Combine co-linear objects that partially overlap
☑ END to END - Combine co-linear objects when aligned end to end

[OK]   [Close]   [Help]

Delete Duplicate Objects (Express Tool)

The Delete Duplicate Objects command will remove lines, arcs, and circles that sit exactly on top of one another. In poorly executed Auto-CAD drawings, multiple lines are drawn exactly on top of one another. This can significantly increase drawing editing time.

· Type the command **OVERKILL** and press **ENTER**.
· Using the mouse, select the objects you want to check for duplicates. In most cases, you want to check the entire drawing. Type **ALL** and press **ENTER**. Press **ENTER** one more time.
· The Overkill dialog box will open. Select your desired settings and **CLICK OK**. The standard settings are shown to the left.
· You have successfully cleaned your drawing of duplicate objects.

Layer Off (Express Tool)

The **LAYOFF** command allows you to turn off layers by selecting objects. If you select an object on the A-DOOR layer, the A-DOOR layer will be turned off.

· Type the command **LAYOFF** and press **ENTER**.
· Using the mouse, select objects on layers you want to turn off.
· Press **ENTER** to end the command.

Turn On All Layers (Express Tool)

The **LAYON** command turns on all layers.

· Type the command **LAYON** and press **ENTER**. All layers in the current drawing are turned on.

Layer Isolate

The **LAYISO** command allows you to visually isolate layers by selecting specific objects on those layers. If you isolate the A-DOOR layer, all layers will be turned off except the A-DOOR layer.

· Type the command **LAYISO** and press **ENTER**.
· Using the mouse, select objects on layers you want to isolate. You may isolate several layers.
· Press **ENTER** to end the command and isolate the selected layers.

Layer Freeze (Express Tool)

The **LAYFRZ** command allows you to freeze layers by selecting objects. If you select an object on the A-DOOR layer, the A-DOOR layer will be frozen. When a layer is frozen, all objects on that layer are not visible and cannot be modified.

· Type the command **LAYFRZ** and press **ENTER**.
· Using the mouse, select objects on layers you want to freeze.
· Press **ENTER** to end the command.

Thaw All Layers (Express Tool)

The **LAYTHW** command allows you to thaw all layers.

· Type the command **LAYTHW** and press **ENTER**. All layers in the current drawing are thawed.

Layer Lock (Express Tool)

The **LAYLCK** command allows you to lock layers by selecting objects. If you select an object on the A-DOOR layer, the A-DOOR layer will be locked. When a layer is locked, all objects on that layer are visible but cannot be modified.

· Type the command **LAYLCK** and press **ENTER**.
· Using the mouse, select an object on the layer you want to lock. The layer is locked and the command ends.

Layer Unlock (Express Tool)

The **LAYULK** command allows you to unlock layers by selecting objects. If you select an object on the A-DOOR layer, the A-DOOR layer will be unlocked.

· Type the command **LAYULK** and press **ENTER**.
· Using the mouse, select an object on the layer you want to unlock. The layer is unlocked and the command ends.

Layer Delete (Express Tool)

The **LAYDEL** command allows you to delete layers (and all objects on those layers) by selecting objects on those layers. If you select an object on the A-DOOR layer, the A-DOOR layer will be deleted (along with all objects on this layer).

· Type the command **LAYDEL** and press **ENTER**.
· Using the mouse, select an object on the layer you want to delete.
· Press **ENTER** when you are finished selecting layers to delete.
· AutoCAD warns, *"You are about to permanently delete layer window from this drawing."* Type the letter **Y** and press **ENTER** to delete the selected layers.

Layer Merge (Express Tool)

The **LAYMRG** command allows you to merge one or more layers onto another layer in your drawing. You could merge the DOOR layer into the A-DOOR layer.

- Type the command **LAYMRG** and press **ENTER**.
- **STEP 1**: Using the mouse, select an object on the layer(s) you want to merge from.
- Press **ENTER** when you are finished selecting layers.
- **STEP 2**: Using the mouse, select an object on the layer you want to merge to.
- AutoCAD warns, "*You are about to permanently merge layer door into layer a-door.*" Type the letter **Y** and press **ENTER** to merge the selected layers.

Layer: A-DOOR

Layer: DOOR

Layer: A-DOOR

Layer: A-DOOR

Learning Exercise

In this exercise, you will clean your drawing and become more familiar with the routine maintenance AutoCAD drawings require. Do not forget to save your drawing frequently when cleaning your drawing. AutoCAD has been known to crash while trying to fix a problem. Frequent saves will ensure that you have an up-to-date drawing when AutoCAD does crash.

Open Your Drawing

· Open AutoCAD.
· Open the drawing you created in the previous chapter:
  DDFD-EAMES.DWG

Cleaning Your Drawing

Complete the following commands to clean your drawing and to remove any extra or potentially corrupt information.

· Set the current layer to **0.**
· **UNLOCK** all layers in your drawing.
· Turn **ON** and **THAW** all layers in your drawing.

· Run the **AUDIT** command to check for any file errors in your drawing.
· **SAVE** your drawing.

· Use the **MATCHPROP** command to fix any lines that are on an incorrect layer.
· Run the **FLATTEN** command to adjust all the Z coordinates in your drawing to 0".
· **SAVE** your drawing.

· Run the **OVERKILL** command to delete any duplicate lines or objects.
· **SAVE** your drawing.

· Run the **PURGE** command to remove unused blocks, layers, and linetypes.
· **SAVE** your drawing.

Congratulations, you have completed the learning exercise for this chapter.

CHAPTER 11
Dimensioning Your Drawing

The previous chapters introduced you to the tools that can help you draw more efficiently in AutoCAD when compared to manual drawing. Dimensioning in AutoCAD can save you more drawing time than any other tool about which you have learned. Dimensioning can also cause many headaches if the drawing is not accurate.

In manual drawings, dimensions are based on an overall understanding of the project design. If two walls scale to a little more than 20'-6" apart in your manual drawing, you will probably write the dimension as 20'-6".

In digital drawings, dimensions are based on the information AutoCAD receives as the drawing is created. Digital drawings are often worked on over several weeks or months by multiple designers. This alone creates an environment where errors can find their way into digital drawings. If two walls scale to a little more than 20'-6" apart in AutoCAD, the computer will give you the precise dimension: 20'-6 5/32".

Consider the following questions as you work through this chapter:
· What are Dimension Styles, and how can they help organize the visual appearance of dimensions in your drawings?
· How does the scale of your drawing affect the process of dimensioning your drawing?
· How do digital drawing errors become obvious when dimensioning a drawing in AutoCAD?

Dimension Your Drawing

AutoCAD simplifies the process of adding dimensions to your drawing. By selecting and setting up a specific dimension style, you will ensure that all the dimensions in your drawing are consistent.

Tick Dimension Style

This dimension style is commonly found in hand-drafted design drawings.

- The text used in this dimension style is sanserif and bold.
- The tick marks clearly identify where the dimension starts and stops.
- The extension lines do not touch the lines in the drawing.

- See page 158 to set up this dimension style in your drawings.

Arrow Dimension Style

This dimension style is a modified version of a common style in hand-drafted design drawings.

- The text used in this dimension style is sanserif and bold.
- The arrows clearly identify where the dimension starts and stops.
- The extension lines do not touch the lines in the drawing.

- See page 162 to set up this dimension style in your drawings.

Box Dimension Style

This dimension style is a modernized version unique to AutoCAD design drawings.

- The text used in this dimension style is san-serif and bold.
- The box identifies where the dimension starts and stops.
- The extension lines do not touch the lines in the drawing.

- See page 166 to set up this dimension style in your drawings.

Dot Dimension Style

This dimension style is commonly used to identify distances between column grids.

- The text used in this dimension style is san-serif and bold.
- The dot identifies where the dimension crosses the column grid.
- There are no extension lines.

- See page 170 to set up this dimension style in your drawings.

Dimensioning Walls

· In floor plans, wall dimensions are generally completed in a continuous line. line of dimensions is referred to as a dimension string.

· In the example to the left, the horizontal dimension strings locate the right finish face of all walls and the vertical dimension strings locate the top finish face of all walls. When dimensioning walls, attempt to dimension to a consistent side of all walls.

Dimensioning Corridors

· Critical dimensions such as corridor widths are dimensioned to indicate a clear opening dimension. This helps the builder understand your intentions and dimension priorities during construction.

· You can add the word **CLEAR** or the abbreviation **CLR** after any dimension to indicate a clear opening dimension.

Editing Dimension Text

· To edit dimension text type the command **DDEDIT** and press **ENTER**.
· **CLICK ONCE** on the dimension text that you want to edit.
· Press **ENTER** when you have finished editing the dimension text.

Dimensioning Windows

· Windows are most commonly dimensioned to their centerline.

· The width of a window is rarely dimensioned in floor plans because this information is located in the window schedule.

· Select and use a consistent method to dimension all of the windows in your project.

Dimensioning Doors

· Doors are most commonly dimensioned to their centerline or to the hinge side of the door.

· The width of a door is rarely dimensioned in floor plans because this information is located in the door schedule.

· Select and use a consistent method to dimension all of the doors in your project.

Dimensioning to Structure

· Structural column grids are usually extended beyond the exterior walls and dimensioned outside the building footprint.

· Structural columns are located at the intersection of the structural column grid.

· Structural columns are most commonly dimensioned to the centerline.

· Structural beams are most commonly dimensioned to the top of the beam.

Adding Dimensions to Your Drawing

The Dimension menu contains many dimensioning options. From this menu, you will use **LINEAR**, **ALIGNED**, and **CONTINUE** to complete most dimensioning tasks in AutoCAD.

Horizontal and Vertical Dimensions

Linear dimensions are either horizontal or vertical and are used to dimension most elements in plans, sections, and elevations.

- Type the command **DIMSTYLE** and press **ENTER**.
- Using the mouse, select the appropriate dimension style/scale and click the **SET CURRENT** button. See later sections on adding dimension styles.
- Click the **CLOSE** button.
- Create a new layer in your drawing:
  A-DIM   Color 7
- Set the current layer to **A-DIM**.

- From the **DIMENSION MENU**, select **LINEAR**.
- **Steps 1 and 2**: Using object snaps, precisely select the first and second points of your dimension string.
- **Step 3**: Drag the cursor away from the dimensioned objects to locate or place the dimension string. **CLICK ONCE**.

- If you want to continue your dimension string, select **CONTINUE** from the **DIMENSION MENU**.

Dimension Style Manager

Current Dimstyle: Standard

Dimension lines

Standard

Set Current
New...
Modify...
Override...
Compare...

Close   Help

Aligned Dimensions

Aligned dimension strings are always parallel to the object or wall they are dimensioning. This type of dimension string is helpful in dimensioning the length of non-orthogonal (angled) walls.

- Type the command **DIMSTYLE** and press **ENTER**.
- Using the mouse, select the appropriate dimension style/scale and click the **SET CURRENT** button. See later sections on adding dimension styles.
- Click the **CLOSE** button.
- Create a new layer in your drawing:
  A-DIM   Color 7
- Set the current layer to **A-DIM**.

AutoCAD

File   Edit   View   Insert   Dimension   Tools

Quick Dimension
Linear
Aligned

Leader

Dimension Style

8'-4"

- From the **DIMENSION MENU**, select **ALIGNED**.
- **Steps 1** and **2**: Using object snaps, precisely select the first and second points of your dimension string.
- **Step 3**: Drag the cursor away from the dimensioned objects to locate or place the dimension string. **CLICK ONCE**.

- If you want to continue your dimension string, select **CONTINUE** from the **DIMENSION MENU**.

Angular Dimensions

Angular dimension strings display the angle of a wall relative to the horizontal or vertical planes. This type of dimension string is helpful in dimensioning the angle of non-orthogonal (angled) walls.

- Type the command **DIMSTYLE** and press **ENTER**.
- Using the mouse, select the appropriate dimension style/scale and click the **SET CURRENT** button. See later sections on adding dimension styles.
- Click the **CLOSE** button.
- Create a new layer in your drawing:
  A-DIM   Color 7
- Set the current layer to **A-DIM**.

- From the **DIMENSION MENU**, select **ANGULAR**.
- **Steps 1 and 2**: Select the first line and the second line that define the angle.
- **Step 3**: Drag the cursor away from the dimensioned objects to locate or place the angular dimension string. **CLICK ONCE**.

Adding the Tick Dimension Style

The following pages will guide you through the process of setting up a Tick Dimension Style (pictured left). The scale of your drawing will affect some settings of your dimension style, so it is important that you know the scale of your drawing before proceeding.

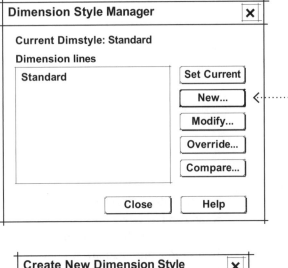

· Create a new layer in your drawing:
  A-DIM   Color 7

· Type the command **DIMSTYLE** and press **ENTER**. This will open the Dimension Style Manager.

· Click the **NEW** button to create a new dimension style.

· Type the style name **TICK-DIM-48** and press the **CONTINUE** button.

· In this example, we are dimensioning a 1/4"=1'-0" drawing with a scale factor of 48. Change the 48 in the style name to match the scale factor for your drawing.

Modify Dimension Style: TICK-DIM-48   [×]

Symbols and Arrows

Arrowheads

First:
[Architectural tick   ▽]

Second:
[Architectural tick   ▽]

Leader:
[Architectural tick   ▽]

Arrow Size:
[1/16"]

Arc length
- ⦿ Preceding dimension text
- ○ Above dimension text
- ○ None

Center marks
- ⦿ None
- ○ Mark
- ○ Line

Radius dimension jog
Jog angle   [45]

[OK]   [Close]   [Help]

Symbols and Arrows Tab

Click once on the Symbols and Arrows tab and make the following modifications:

- Set all Arrowheads to: **ARCHITECTURAL TICK**
- Set Arrow Size to **1/16"**

- Set Center marks to: **NONE**

Modify Dimension Style: TICK-DIM-48   [×]

Lines

Dimension lines

Color: [Byblock   ▽]
Linetype: [Byblock   ▽]
Lineweight: [Byblock   ▽]
Extend beyond ticks: [1/32"]
Baseline spacing: [0"]
Suppress: ☐ Dim line 1   ☐ Dim line 2

Extension lines

Color: [Byblock   ▽]   Extend beyond dim line: [1/32"]
Linetype ext 1: [Byblock   ▽]   Offset from origin: [1/16"]
Linetype ext 2: [Byblock   ▽]
Lineweight: [Byblock   ▽]
Suppress: ☐ Ext line 1   ☐ Ext line 2

[OK]   [Close]   [Help]

Lines Tab

Click once on the Lines tab and make the following modifications:

- Set Extend beyond ticks to: **1/32"**
- Set Baseline spacing to: **0"**

- Set Extend beyond dim line to: **1/32"**
- Set Offset from origin to: **1/16"**

Modify Dimension Style: TICK-DIM-48 ✕

Text

Text appearance

Text style:	Standard ▽
Text color:	Blue ▽
Fill color:	None ▽
Text height:	3/32"
Fraction height scale:	0.6666

☐ Draw frame around text

Text placement

Vertical:	Above ▽
Horizontal:	Centered ▽
Offset from dim line:	1/32"

Text alignment

○ Horizontal
⦿ Aligned with dimension line
○ ISO standard

[OK] [Close] [Help]

Text Tab

Click once on the Text tab and make the following modifications:

- Set the Text style to: **STANDARD**
- Set the Text color to: **BLUE**
- Set the Fill color to: **NONE**
- For construction documents, set the Text height to: **3/32"**
- For presentation drawings, set the Text height between: **1/8"** and **1/4"**

- Set the Fraction height scale to: **0.6666**
- Set the Vertical text placement to: **ABOVE**
- Set the Horizontal text placement to: **CENTERED**
- Set the Offset from dim line to: **1/32"**
- Set the Text alignment to: **ALIGNED WITH DIMENSION LINE**

Modify Dimension Style: TICK-DIM-48 ✕

Fit

Fit options

If there isn't enough room to place both text and arrows inside extension lines, the first thing to move outside the extension lines is:

○ Either text or arrows
○ Arrows
○ Text
○ Both text and arrows
⦿ Always keep text between ext lines

☐ Suppress arrows if they don't fit inside extension lines

Text placement

When text is not in the default position, place it:

○ Beside the dimension line
○ Over dimension line with leader
⦿ Over dimension line without leader

Scale for dimension features

⦿ Use overall scale of: 48
○ Scale dimensions to layout

Fine tuning

☐ Pace text manually
☒ Draw dim line between ext lines

[OK] [Close] [Help]

Fit Tab

Click once on the Fit tab and make the following modifications:

- Set the Fit options to: **ALWAYS KEEP TEXT BETWEEN EXT LINES**
- Set the Text placement to: **OVER DIMENSION LINE WITHOUT LEADER**

- Set the Scale for dimension features to match the scale factor for your drawing. In this example, we are dimensioning a 1/4"=1'-0" drawing with a scale factor of 48.

- In the Fine tuning section, check the option to: **DRAW DIM LINE BETWEEN EXT LINES**

Modify Dimension Style: TICK-DIM-48 ✕

Primary Units

Linear dimensions

Unit format:	Architectural ▽
Precision:	1/16" ▽
Fractional format:	Horizontal ▽
Decimal separator:	
Round off:	0"
Prefix:	
Suffix:	

Measurement scale

Scale factor: 1.000

☐ Apply to layout dimensions only

Zero suppression

☐ Leading   ☒ 0 feet
☐ Trailing   ☐ 0 inches

Angular dimensions

Unit format:	Decimal Degrees ▽
Precision:	0 ▽

Zero suppression

☐ Leading
☐ Trailing

[OK]   [Close]   [Help]

Primary Units Tab

Click once on the Primary Units tab and make the following modifications:

- Set the Unit format to: **ARCHITECTURAL**
- Set the Precision to: **1/16"**
- Set the Fractional format to: **HORIZONTAL**
- Set the Round off to: **0"**

- Set the Measurement scale to: **1.000**
- In the Zero suppression section (linear dimension), check the option: **0 FEET**

Modify Dimension Style: TICK-DIM-48 ✕

Alternate Units

No Changes Required

[OK]   [Close]   [Help]

Alternate Units Tab

No modifications are required for this tab.

Modify Dimension Style: TICK-DIM-48 ✕

Tolerances

No Changes Required

[OK]   [Close]   [Help]

Tolerances Tab

No modifications are required for this tab.

Adding the Arrow Dimension Style
The following pages will guide you through the process of setting up an Arrow Dimension Style (pictured left). The scale of your drawing will affect some settings of your dimension style, so it is important that you know the scale of your drawing before proceeding.

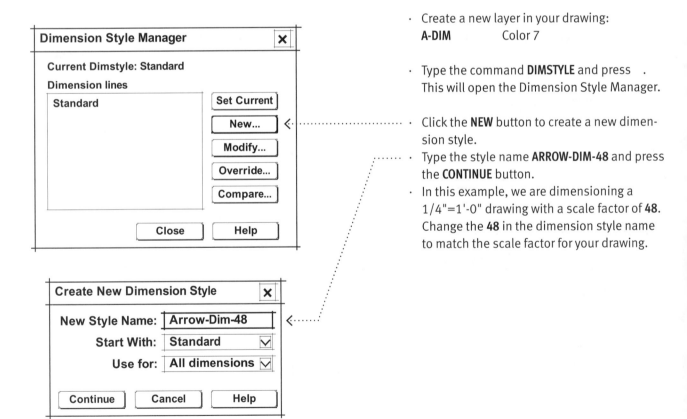

· Create a new layer in your drawing:
A-DIM   Color 7

· Type the command **DIMSTYLE** and press   .
This will open the Dimension Style Manager.

· Click the **NEW** button to create a new dimension style.

· Type the style name **ARROW-DIM-48** and press the **CONTINUE** button.

· In this example, we are dimensioning a 1/4"=1'-0" drawing with a scale factor of **48**. Change the **48** in the dimension style name to match the scale factor for your drawing.

Modify Dimension Style: ARROW-DIM-48 [×]

Lines

Dimension lines

Color:	Byblock	▽
Linetype:	Byblock	▽
Lineweight:	Byblock	▽
Extend beyond ticks:	0"	
Baseline spacing:	0"	
Suppress:	☐ Dim line 1 ☐ Dim line 2	

Extension lines

Color:	Byblock	▽	Extend beyond dim line:	1/32"
Linetype ext 1:	Byblock	▽	Offset from origin:	1/16"
Linetype ext 2:	Byblock	▽
Lineweight:	Byblock	▽
Suppress:	☐ Ext line 1 ☐ Ext line 2

[OK] [Close] [Help]

Lines Tab
Click once on the Lines tab and make the following modifications:

· Set Extend beyond ticks to: **0"**
· Set Baseline spacing to: **0"**

· Set Extend beyond dim line to: **1/32"**
· Set Offset from origin to: **1/16"**

Modify Dimension Style: ARROW-DIM-48 [×]

Symbols and Arrows

Arrowheads

First:
| Closed Filled (Arrow) | ▽ |

Second:
| Closed Filled (Arrow) | ▽ |

Leader:
| Closed Filled (Arrow) | ▽ |

Arrow Size:
| 3/32" |

Center marks
- ⦿ None
- ○ Mark
- ○ Line

Arc length
- ⦿ Preceding dimension text
- ○ Above dimension text
- ○ None

Radius dimension jog
Jog angle | 45 |

[OK] [Close] [Help]

Symbols and Arrows Tab
Click once on the Symbols and Arrows tab and make the following modifications:

· Set all Arrowheads to: **CLOSED FILLED (ARROW)**
· Set Arrow Size to: **3/32"**

· Set Center marks to: **NONE**

Modify Dimension Style: ARROW-DIM-48 ✕

Text

Text appearance

Text style:	Standard ▼
Text color:	Blue ▼
Fill color:	None ▼
Text height:	3/32"
Fraction height scale:	0.6666

☐ Draw frame around text

Text placement

Vertical:	Above ▼
Horizontal:	Centered ▼
Offset from dim line:	1/32"

Text alignment

○ Horizontal
● Aligned with dimension line
○ ISO standard

[OK] [Close] [Help]

Text Tab

Click once on the Text tab and make the following modifications:

- Set the Text style to: **STANDARD**
- Set the Text color to: **BLUE**
- Set the Fill color to: **NONE**
- For construction documents, set the Text height to: **3/32"**
- For presentation drawings, set the Text height between: **1/8"** and **1/4"**

- Set the Fraction height scale to: **0.6666**
- Set the Vertical text placement to: **ABOVE**
- Set the Horizontal text placement to: **CENTERED**
- Set the Offset from dim line to: **1/32"**
- Set the Text alignment to: **ALIGNED WITH DIMENSION LINE**

Modify Dimension Style: ARROW-DIM-48 ✕

Fit

Fit options

If there isn't enough room to place both text and arrows inside extension lines, the first thing to move outside the extension lines is:

○ Either text or arrows
○ Arrows
○ Text
○ Both text and arrows
● Always keep text between ext lines
☐ Suppress arrows if they don't fit inside extension lines

Text placement

When text is not in the default position, place it:

○ Beside the dimension line
○ Over dimension line with leader
● Over dimension line without leader

Scale for dimension features

● Use overall scale of: 48
○ Scale dimensions to layout

Fine tuning

☐ Pace text manually
☒ Draw dim line between ext lines

[OK] [Close] [Help]

Fit Tab

Click once on the Fit tab and make the following modifications:

- Set the Fit options to: **ALWAYS KEEP TEXT BETWEEN EXT LINES**
- Set the Text placement to: **OVER DIMENSION LINE WITHOUT LEADER**

- Set the Scale for dimension features to match the scale factor for your drawing. In this example, we are dimensioning a 1/4"=1'-0" drawing with a scale factor of 48.

- In the Fine tuning section, check the option to: **DRAW DIM LINE BETWEEN EXT LINES**

Modify Dimension Style: ARROW-DIM-48   ☒

Primary Units

Linear dimensions

Unit format:	Architectural ▽
Precision:	1/16" ▽
Fractional format:	Horizontal ▽
Decimal separator:	
Round off:	0"
Prefix:	
Suffix:	

Measurement scale

Scale factor: 1.000

☐ Apply to layout dimensions only

Zero suppression

☐ Leading   ☒ 0 feet

☐ Trailing   ☐ 0 inches

Angular dimensions

Unit format:	Decimal Degrees ▽
Precision:	0 ▽

Zero suppression

☐ Leading

☐ Trailing

[OK]   [Close]   [Help]

Primary Units Tab

Click once on the Primary Units tab and make the following modifications:

- Set the Unit format to: **ARCHITECTURAL**
- Set the Precision to: **1/16"**
- Set the Fractional format to: **HORIZONTAL**
- Set the Round off to: **0"**

- Set the Measurement scale to: **1.000**
- In the Zero suppression section (linear dimension), check the option: **0 FEET**

Modify Dimension Style: ARROW-DIM-48   ☒

Alternate Units

No Changes Required

[OK]   [Close]   [Help]

Alternate Units Tab

No modifications are required for this tab.

Modify Dimension Style: ARROW-DIM-48   ☒

Tolerances

No Changes Required

[OK]   [Close]   [Help]

Tolerances Tab

No modifications are required for this tab.

Adding the Box Dimension Style

The following pages will guide you through the process of setting up a Box Dimension Style (pictured left). The scale of your drawing will affect some settings of your dimension style, so it is important that you know the scale of your drawing before proceeding.

· Create a new layer in your drawing:
  A-DIM   Color 7

· Type the command **DIMSTYLE** and press **ENTER**. This will open the Dimension Style Manager.

· Click the **NEW** button to create a new dimension style.

· Type the style name **BOX-DIM-48** and press the **CONTINUE** button.

· In this example, we are dimensioning a 1/4"=1'-0" drawing with a scale factor of **48**. Change the **48** in the dimension style name to match the **SCALE FACTOR** for your drawing.

Modify Dimension Style: BOX-DIM-48 ☒

Lines

Dimension lines

Color:	Byblock ▽
Linetype:	Byblock ▽
Lineweight:	Byblock ▽
Extend beyond ticks:	0"
Baseline spacing:	0"
Suppress:	☐ Dim line 1 ☐ Dim line 2

Extension lines

Color:	Byblock ▽	Extend beyond dim line: 1/32"
Linetype ext 1:	Byblock ▽	Offset from origin: 1/16"
Linetype ext 2:	Byblock ▽	
Lineweight:	Byblock ▽	
Suppress:	☐ Ext line 1 ☐ Ext line 2	

[OK]   [Close]   [Help]

Lines Tab
Click once on the Lines tab and make the following modifications:

- Set Extend beyond ticks to: **0"**
- Set Baseline spacing to: **0"**

- Set Extend beyond dim line to: **1/32"**
- Set Offset from origin to: **1/16"**

Modify Dimension Style: BOX-DIM-48 ☒

Symbols and Arrows

Arrowheads

First:
Box Filled ▽

Second:
Box Filled ▽

Leader:
Box Filled ▽

Arrow Size:
1/32"

Center marks
- ⦿ None
- ◯ Mark
- ◯ Line

Arc length
- ⦿ Preceding dimension text
- ◯ Above dimension text
- ◯ None

Radius dimension jog
Jog angle 45

[OK]   [Close]   [Help]

Symbols and Arrows Tab
Click once on the Symbols and Arrows tab and make the following modifications:

- Set all Arrowheads to: **BOX FILLED**
- Set Arrow Size to: **1/32"**

- Set Center marks to: **NONE**

Modify Dimension Style: BOX-DIM-48 ☒

Text

Text appearance

Text style:	Standard ▽
Text color:	Blue ▽
Fill color:	None ▽
Text height:	3/32"
Fraction height scale:	0.6666
☐ Draw frame around text	

Text placement

Vertical:	Above ▽
Horizontal:	Centered ▽
Offset from dim line:	1/32"

Text alignment

- ○ Horizontal
- ◉ Aligned with dimension line
- ○ ISO standard

[OK] [Close] [Help]

Text Tab

Click once on the Text tab and make the following modifications:

- Set the Text style to: **STANDARD**
- Set the Text color to: **BLUE**
- Set the Fill color to: **NONE**
- For construction documents, set the Text height to: **3/32"**
- For presentation drawings, set the Text height between: **1/8"** and **1/4"**

- Set the Fraction height scale to: **0.6666**
- Set the Vertical text placement to: **ABOVE**
- Set the Horizontal text placement to: **CENTERED**
- Set the Offset from dim line to: **1/32"**
- Set the Text alignment to: **ALIGNED WITH DIMENSION LINE**

Modify Dimension Style: BOX-DIM-48 ☒

Fit

Fit options

If there isn't enough room to place both text and arrows inside extension lines, the first thing to move outside the extension lines is:

- ○ Either text or arrows
- ○ Arrows
- ○ Text
- ○ Both text and arrows
- ◉ Always keep text between ext lines
- ☐ Suppress arrows if they don't fit inside extension lines

Text placement

When text is not in the default position, place it:

- ○ Beside the dimension line
- ○ Over dimension line with leader
- ◉ Over dimension line without leader

Scale for dimension features

- ◉ Use overall scale of: 48
- ○ Scale dimensions to layout

Fine tuning

- ☐ Pace text manually
- ☒ Draw dim line between ext lines

[OK] [Close] [Help]

Fit Tab

Click once on the Fit tab and make the following modifications:

- Set the Fit options to: **ALWAYS KEEP TEXT BETWEEN EXT LINES**
- Set the Text placement to: **OVER DIMENSION LINE WITHOUT LEADER**

- Set the Scale for dimension features to match the scale factor for your drawing. In this example, we are dimensioning a 1/4"=1'-0" drawing with a scale factor of 48.

- In the Fine tuning section, check the option to: **DRAW DIM LINE BETWEEN EXT LINES**

Modify Dimension Style: BOX-DIM-48

Primary Units

Linear dimensions

Unit format: Architectural

Precision: 1/16"

Fractional format: Horizontal

Decimal separator:

Round off: 0"

Prefix:

Suffix:

Measurement scale

Scale factor: 1.000

☐ Apply to layout dimensions only

Zero suppression
☐ Leading ☒ 0 feet
☐ Trailing ☐ 0 inches

Angular dimensions

Unit format: Decimal Degrees

Precision: 0

Zero suppression
☐ Leading
☐ Trailing

[OK] [Close] [Help]

Primary Units Tab

Click once on the Primary Units tab and make the following modifications:

· Set the Unit format to: **ARCHITECTURAL**
· Set the Unit precision to: **1/16"**
· Set the Fractional format to: **HORIZONTAL**
· Set the Round off to: **0"**

· Set the Measurement scale to: **1.000**
· In the Zero suppression section (linear dimension), check the option: **0 FEET**

Modify Dimension Style: BOX-DIM-48

Alternate Units

No Changes Required

[OK] [Close] [Help]

Alternate Units Tab

No modifications are required for this tab.

Modify Dimension Style: BOX-DIM-48

Tolerances

No Changes Required

[OK] [Close] [Help]

Tolerances Tab

No modifications are required for this tab.

Adding the Dot Dimension Style

The following pages will guide you through the process of setting up a Dot Dimension Style (pictured left). The scale of your drawing will affect some settings of your dimension style, so it is important that you know the scale of your drawing before proceeding.

· Create a new layer in your drawing:
A-DIM   Color 7

· Type the command **DIMSTYLE** and press **ENTER**. This will open the Dimension Style Manager.

· Click the **NEW** button to create a new dimension style.

· Type the style name **DOT-DIM-48** and press the **CONTINUE** button.

· In this example, we are dimensioning a 1/4"=1'-0" drawing with a scale factor of **48**. Change the **48** in the dimension style name to match the scale factor for your drawing.

Modify Dimension Style: DOT-DIM-48 ✕

Lines

Dimension lines

Color:	Byblock	▽
Linetype:	Byblock	▽
Lineweight:	Byblock	▽
Extend beyond ticks:		0"
Baseline spacing:		0"
Suppress:	☐ Dim line 1	☐ Dim line 2

Extension lines

Color:	Byblock	Extend beyond dim line:	1/32"
Linetype ext 1:	Byblock	Offset from origin:	1/16"
Linetype ext 2:	Byblock		
Lineweight:	Byblock		
Suppress:	☒ Ext line 1	☒ Ext line 2	

[OK] [Close] [Help]

Lines Tab
Click once on the Lines tab and make the following modifications:

- Set Extend beyond ticks to: **0"**
- Set Baseline spacing to: **0"**

- Set Extend beyond dim line to: **1/32"**
- Set Offset from origin to: **1/16"**

- Suppress: **EXT LINE 1**
- Suppress: **EXT LINE 2**

Modify Dimension Style: DOT-DIM-48 ✕

Symbols and Arrows

Arrowheads

First:
| Dot | ▽ |

Second:
| Dot | ▽ |

Leader:
| Dot | ▽ |

Arrow Size:
| 1/16" |

Center marks
- ◉ None
- ◯ Mark
- ◯ Line

Arc length
- ◉ Preceding dimension text
- ◯ Above dimension text
- ◯ None

Radius dimension jog
Jog angle | 45 |

[OK] [Close] [Help]

Symbols and Arrows Tab
Click once on the Symbols and Arrows tab and make the following modifications:

- Set all Arrowheads to: **DOT**
- Set Arrow Size to: **1/16"**

- Set Center marks to: **NONE**

Text Tab

Click once on the Text tab and make the following modifications:

- Set the Text style to: **STANDARD**
- Set the Text color to: **BLUE**
- Set the Fill color to: **NONE**
- For construction documents, set the Text height to: **3/32"**
- For presentation drawings, set the Text height between: **1/8"** and **1/4"**

- Set the Fraction height scale to: **0.6666**
- Set the Vertical text placement to: **ABOVE**
- Set the Horizontal text placement to: **CENTERED**
- Set the Offset from dim line to: **1/32"**
- Set the Text alignment to: **ALIGNED WITH DIMENSION LINE**

Fit Tab

Click once on the Fit tab and make the following modifications:

- Set the Fit options to: **ALWAYS KEEP TEXT BETWEEN EXT LINES**
- Set the Text placement to: **OVER DIMENSION LINE WITHOUT LEADER**

- Set the Scale for dimension features to match the scale factor for your drawing. In this example, we are dimensioning a 1/4"=1'-0" drawing with a scale factor of 48.

- In the Fine tuning section, check the option to: **DRAW DIM LINE BETWEEN EXT LINES**

Modify Dimension Style: DOT-DIM-48 ⊠

Primary Units

Linear dimensions

Unit format:	Architectural ▽
Precision:	1/16" ▽
Fractional format:	Horizontal ▽
Decimal separator:	
Round off:	0"
Prefix:	
Suffix:	

Measurement scale

Scale factor: 1.000

☐ Apply to layout dimensions only

Zero suppression

☐ Leading ⊠ 0 feet

☐ Trailing ☐ 0 inches

Angular dimensions

Unit format:	Decimal Degrees ▽
Precision:	0 ▽

Zero suppression

☐ Leading

☐ Trailing

[OK] [Close] [Help]

Primary Units Tab

Click once on the Primary Units tab and make
the following modifications:

- Set the Unit format to: **ARCHITECTURAL**
- Set the Precision to: **1/16"**
- Set the Fractional format to: **HORIZONTAL**
- Set the Round off to: **0"**

- Set the Measurement scale to: **1.000**
- In the Zero suppression section (linear
  dimension), check the option: **0 FEET**

Modify Dimension Style: DOT-DIM-48 ⊠

Alternate Units

No Changes Required

[OK] [Close] [Help]

Alternate Units Tab

No modifications are required for this tab.

Modify Dimension Style: DOT-DIM-48 ⊠

Tolerances

No Changes Required

[OK] [Close] [Help]

Tolerances Tab

No modifications are required for this tab.

Learning Exercise

In this exercise, you will set up a dimension style and add dimensions to your floor plan.

Open Your Drawing
- Open AutoCAD.
- Open the drawing you created in the previous chapter:
  DDFD-EAMES.DWG

Creating Your Layers

Create the following layers.

- **A-DIM**   Color 7
- Set the current layer to **A-DIM.**

Adding a Dimension Style

- Using the guides in this chapter, create the Tick dimension style in your drawing. Name this dimension style **TICK-DIM-96**.
- In the Fit tab, set the overall scale to match the scale factor for 1/8"=1'-0".
- Set the current dimension style to: **TICK-DIM-96**.

- Save your drawing.

Dimensioning Your Drawing

· Using the various dimension commands, add dimensions to your drawing to match the drawing above.

· Save your drawing.

Congratulations, you have completed the learning exercise for this chapter.

CHAPTER 12
Text Leaders

As you develop design drawings you will increasingly need to add notes to your drawings. At the same time, you may also find that there is not enough space inside your drawing to include the amount of text required to communicate your design idea.

The Text Leader command in AutoCAD allows you to draw a leader line with an arrow or dot on one end and multiline text on the other end. This method of adding notes to drawings is used primarily in construction drawings.

Notes/Text Leaders

Like dimensions, AutoCAD simplifies the process of adding notes (text leaders) to your drawing. By selecting and setting up a specific dimension style, you will ensure that the notes in your drawing are consistent.

Dot Text Leaders

This dimension leader style is commonly used to note surfaces in plan, section, elevation, and details.

· The text used in this dimension style is san-serif and bold.
· The dot is clearly located on the surface noted.
· The leader lines are parallel to each other and, when possible, cross other lines in the drawing at an angle.

· See page 184 to set up this dimension style in your drawings.

Arrow Text Leaders

This dimension leader style is commonly used to note objects in plan, section, elevation, and details.

· The text used in this dimension style is san-serif and bold.
· The arrow points directly to the object noted.
· The leader lines are parallel to each other and cross other lines in the drawing at an angle.

· See page 170 to set up this dimension style in your drawings.

Adding Notes to Your Drawing

The Dimension menu contains several dimensioning options. From this menu, you will use **LEADER** to complete most of the note tasks in your AutoCAD drawing.

LIGHT SWITCH

Text Leader

Leaders always start at the object or surface and continue off the drawing at an angle.

- Type the command **DIMSTYLE** and press **ENTER**.
- Using the mouse, select the appropriate dimension leader style/scale and click the **SET CURRENT** button.
- Click the **CLOSE** button.
- Create a new layer in your drawing
  A-NOTE   Color 5
- Set the current layer to **A-NOTE**

- From the **DIMENSION MENU**, select **LEADER**.
- **Step 1**: Using object snaps, precisely select the first point of your leader.
- **Step 2**: Turn **ORTHO OFF**. Type **‹-60** and press **ENTER**. As you drag the cursor, notice that AutoCAD has locked your line to a 60-degree angle.
- Drag the cursor away from the object and **CLICK** to locate the end of the angled leader.

- **Step 3**: Turn **ORTHO ON**. Drag the cursor in the horizontal direction and **CLICK** to locate the end of the leader.
- Press **ENTER** on the keyboard.
- **Step 4**: Type the note for this leader. When you are finished, press **ENTER TWICE**.

Tip: If you do not want to start from scratch, try copying leaders between your drawings.

1'-0"

4'-0"

1'-6"

ROOM 100

A/V FIRE ALARM
LIGHT SWITCH
DUPLEX OUTLET

Adding the Arrow Text Leader Style
The following pages will guide you through the process of setting up an Arrow Text Leader Style (pictured left). The scale of your drawing will affect some settings of your dimension style, so it is important that you know the scale of your drawing before proceeding.

Dimension Style Manager

Current Dimstyle: Standard

Dimension lines

Standard

- Set Current
- New...
- Modify...
- Override...
- Compare...
- Close
- Help

Create New Dimension Style

New Style Name: Arrow-Note-48
Start With: Standard
Use for: All dimensions

- Continue
- Cancel
- Help

· Create a new layer in your drawing:
  A-NOTE   Color 5

· Type the command **DIMSTYLE** and press **ENTER**. This will open the Dimension Style Manager.

· Click the **NEW** button to create a new dimension style.
· Type the style name **ARROW-NOTE-48** and press the **CONTINUE** button.

· In this example, we are dimensioning a 1/4"=1'-0" drawing with a scale factor of **48**. Change the **48** in the dimension style name to match the scale factor for your drawing.

Modify Dimension Style: ARROW-NOTE-48   ✕

Lines

Dimension lines

Color:	Byblock ▽
Linetype:	Byblock ▽
Lineweight:	Byblock ▽
Extend beyond ticks:	0"
Baseline spacing:	0"
Suppress:	☐ Dim line 1 ☐ Dim line 2

Extension lines

Color:	Byblock ▽	Extend beyond dim line:	1/16"
Linetype ext 1:	Byblock ▽	Offset from origin:	1/16"
Linetype ext 2:	Byblock ▽		
Lineweight:	Byblock ▽		
Suppress:	☐ Ext line 1 ☐ Ext line 2		

[OK]   [Close]   [Help]

Lines Tab
Click once on the Lines tab and make the following modifications:

- Set Extend beyond ticks to: **0"**
- Set Baseline spacing to: **0"**

- Set Extend beyond dim line to: **1/16"**
- Set Offset from origin to: **1/16"**

Modify Dimension Style: ARROW-NOTE-48   ✕

Symbols and Arrows

Arrowheads

First:
Closed Filled (Arrow) ▽

Second:
Closed Filled (Arrow) ▽

Leader:
Closed Filled (Arrow) ▽

Arrow Size:
1/8"

Center marks
- ○ None
- ○ Mark
- ● Line

Arc length
- ● Preceding dimension text
- ○ Above dimension text
- ○ None

Radius dimension jog

Jog angle   45

[OK]   [Close]   [Help]

Symbols and Arrows Tab
Click once on the Symbols and Arrows tab and make the following modifications:

- Set all Arrowheads to: **CLOSED FILLED (ARROW)**
- Set Arrow Size to: **1/8"**

- Set Center marks to: **LINE**

Modify Dimension Style: ARROW-NOTE-48

Text

Text appearance

Text style:	Standard ▽
Text color:	Blue ▽
Fill color:	None ▽
Text height:	3/32"
Fraction height scale:	0.6666

☐ Draw frame around text

Text placement

Vertical:	Centered ▽
Horizontal:	Centered ▽
Offset from dim line:	1/32"

Text alignment

○ Horizontal

◉ Aligned with dimension line

○ ISO standard

[OK] [Close] [Help]

Text Tab

Click once on the Text tab and make the following modifications:

· Set the Text style to: **STANDARD**
· Set the Text color to: **BLUE**
· Set the Fill color to: **NONE**
· For construction documents, set the Text height to: **3/32"**
· For presentation drawings, set the Text height between: **1/8"** and **1/4"**

· Set the Fraction height scale to: **0.6666**
· Set the Vertical text placement to: **CENTERED**
· Set the Horizontal text placement to: **CENTERED**
· Set the Offset from dim line to: **1/32"**
· Set the Text alignment to: **ALIGNED WITH DIMENSION LINE**

Modify Dimension Style: ARROW-NOTE-48

Fit

Fit options

If there isn't enough room to place both text and arrows inside extension lines, the first thing to move outside the extension lines is:

○ Either text or arrows

○ Arrows

○ Text

○ Both text and arrows

◉ Always keep text between ext lines

☐ Suppress arrows if they don't fit inside extension lines

Text placement

When text is not in the default position, place it:

○ Beside the dimension line

○ Over dimension line with leader

◉ Over dimension line without leader

Scale for dimension features

◉ Use overall scale of: 48

○ Scale dimensions to layout

Fine tuning

☐ Pace text manually

☒ Draw dim line between ext lines

[OK] [Close] [Help]

Fit Tab

Click once on the Fit tab and make the following modifications:

· Set the Fit options to: **ALWAYS KEEP TEXT BETWEEN EXT LINES**
· Set the text placement to: **OVER DIMENSION LINE WITHOUT LEADER**

· Set the Scale for dimension features to match the scale factor for your drawing. In this example, we are dimensioning a 1/4"=1'-0" drawing with a scale factor of 48.

· In the Fine tuning section, check the option to: **DRAW DIM LINE BETWEEN EXT LINES**

Modify Dimension Style: ARROW-NOTE-48

Primary Units

Linear dimensions

Unit format:	Architectural ▼
Precision:	1/16" ▼
Fractional format:	Horizontal ▼
Decimal separator:	
Round off:	0"
Prefix:	
Suffix:	

Measurement scale

Scale factor: 1.000
☐ Apply to layout dimensions only

Zero suppression
☐ Leading   ☒ 0 feet
☐ Trailing   ☐ 0 inches

Angular dimensions

Unit format:	Decimal Degrees ▼
Precision:	0 ▼

Zero suppression
☐ Leading
☐ Trailing

[OK]   [Close]   [Help]

Primary Units Tab

Click once on the Primary Units tab and make the following modifications:

- Set the Unit format to: **ARCHITECTURAL**
- Set the Precision to: **1/16"**
- Set the Fractional format to: **HORIZONTAL**
- Set the Round off to: **0"**

- Set the Measurement scale to: **1.000**
- In the Zero suppression section (linear dimension), check the option: **0 FEET**

Modify Dimension Style: ARROW-NOTE-48

Alternate Units

No Changes Required

[OK]   [Close]   [Help]

Alternate Units Tab

No modifications are required for this tab.

Modify Dimension Style: ARROW-NOTE-48

Tolerances

No Changes Required

[OK]   [Close]   [Help]

Tolerances Tab

No modifications are required for this tab.

Adding the Dot Text Leader Style

The following pages will guide you through the process of setting up a Dot Text Leader Style. The scale of your drawing will affect some settings of your dimension style, so it is important that you know the scale of your drawing before proceeding.

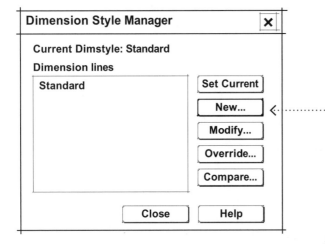

- Create a new layer in your drawing:
  A-NOTE   Color 5

- Type the command **DIMSTYLE** and press **ENTER**. This will open the Dimension Style Manager.

- Click the **NEW** button to create a new dimension style.

- Type the style name **DOT-NOTE-48** and press the **CONTINUE** button.

- In this example, we are dimensioning a 1/4"=1'-0" drawing with a scale factor of **48**. Change the **48** in the dimension style name to match the scale factor for your drawing.

Modify Dimension Style: DOT-NOTE-48

Lines

Dimension lines

Color:	Byblock
Linetype:	Byblock
Lineweight:	Byblock
Extend beyond ticks:	0"
Baseline spacing:	0"
Suppress:	☐ Dim line 1 ☐ Dim line 2

Extension lines

Color:	Byblock	Extend beyond dim line:	1/16"
Linetype ext 1:	Byblock	Offset from origin:	1/16"
Linetype ext 2:	Byblock		
Lineweight:	Byblock		
Suppress:	☐ Ext line 1 ☐ Ext line 2		

OK   **Close**   **Help**

Lines Tab

Click once on the Lines tab and make the following modifications:

- Set Extend beyond ticks to: **0"**
- Set Baseline spacing to: **0"**

- Set Extend beyond dim line to: **1/16"**
- Set Offset from origin to: **1/16"**

Modify Dimension Style: DOT-NOTE-48

Symbols and Arrows

Arrowheads

First:
Dot

Second:
Dot

Leader:
Dot

Arrow Size:
1/16"

Center marks
- ○ None
- ○ Mark
- ● Line

Arc length
- ● Preceding dimension text
- ○ Above dimension text
- ○ None

Radius dimension jog

Jog angle   45

OK   **Close**   **Help**

Symbols and Arrows Tab

Click once on the Symbols and Arrows tab and make the following modifications:

- Set all Arrowheads to: **DOT**
- Set Arrow Size to: **1/16"**

- Set Center marks to: **LINE**

Modify Dimension Style: DOT-NOTE-48 ✕

Text

Text appearance

Text style:	Standard ▽
Text color:	Blue ▽
Fill color:	None ▽
Text height:	3/32"
Fraction height scale:	0.6666

☐ Draw frame around text

Text placement

Vertical:	Centered ▽
Horizontal:	Centered ▽
Offset from dim line:	1/32"

Text alignment

○ Horizontal
◉ Aligned with dimension line
○ ISO standard

| OK | Close | Help |

Text Tab

Click once on the Text tab and make the following modifications:

· Set the Text style to: **STANDARD**
· Set the Text color to: **BLUE**
· Set the Fill color to: **NONE**
· For construction documents, set the Text height to: **3/32"**
· For presentation drawings, set the Text height between: **1/8"** and **1/4"**

· Set the Fraction height scale to: **0.6666**
· Set the Vertical text placement to: **CENTERED**
· Set the Horizontal text placement to: **CENTERED**
· Set the Offset from dim line to: **1/32"**
· Set the Text alignment to: **ALIGNED WITH DIMENSION LINE**

Modify Dimension Style: DOT-NOTE-48 ✕

Fit

Fit options

If there isn't enough room to place both text and arrows inside extension lines, the first thing to move outside the extension lines is:

○ Either text or arrows
○ Arrows
○ Text
○ Both text and arrows
◉ Always keep text between ext lines

☐ Suppress arrows if they don't fit inside extension lines

Text placement

When text is not in the default position, place it:

○ Beside the dimension line
○ Over dimension line with leader
◉ Over dimension line without leader

Scale for dimension features

◉ Use overall scale of: 48
○ Scale dimensions to layout

Fine tuning

☐ Pace text manually
☒ Draw dim line between ext lines

| OK | Close | Help |

Fit Tab

Click once on the Fit tab and make the following modifications:

· Set the Fit options to: **ALWAYS KEEP TEXT BETWEEN EXT LINES**
· Set the Text placement to: **OVER DIMENSION LINE WITHOUT LEADER**

· Set the Scale for dimension features to match the scale factor for your drawing. In this example, we are dimensioning a 1/4"=1'-0" drawing with a scale factor of 48.

· In the Fine tuning section, check the option to: **DRAW DIM LINE BETWEEN EXT LINES**

Modify Dimension Style: DOT-NOTE-48 ✕

Primary Units

Linear dimensions

Unit format:	Architectural ▽
Precision:	1/16" ▽
Fractional format:	Horizontal ▽
Decimal separator:	
Round off:	0"
Prefix:	
Suffix:	

Measurement scale

Scale factor: 1.000

☐ Apply to layout dimensions only

Angular dimensions

Unit format:	Decimal Degrees ▽
Precision:	0 ▽

Zero suppression
- ☐ Leading ☒ 0 feet
- ☐ Trailing ☐ 0 inches

Zero suppression
- ☐ Leading
- ☐ Trailing

[OK] [Close] [Help]

Primary Units Tab
Click once on the Primary Units tab and make the following modifications:

- Set the Unit format to: **ARCHITECTURAL**
- Set the Precision to: **1/16"**
- Set the Fractional format to: **HORIZONTAL**
- Set the Round off to: **0"**

- Set the Measurement scale to: **1.000**
- In the Zero suppression section (linear dimension), check the option: **0 FEET**

Modify Dimension Style: DOT-NOTE-48 ✕

Alternate Units

No Changes Required

[OK] [Close] [Help]

Alternate Units Tab
No modifications are required for this tab.

Modify Dimension Style: DOT-NOTE-48 ✕

Tolerances

No Changes Required

[OK] [Close] [Help]

Tolerances Tab
No modifications are required for this tab.

Learning Exercises

There are several exercises on our website, http://www.fairchildbooks .com/book.cms?bookId=179, that allow you to test your understanding of text leaders in AutoCAD. In these exercises you will use text leaders to add notes to interior elevations and floor plans. Look inside the Chapter 12 folder for these exercises.

CHAPTER 13
Drawing Symbols and Attributed Text

In previous chapters you learned the advantages of using blocks to organize repeating elements such as furniture and doors in your drawing. There are also graphic symbols used in design drawings that communicate the relationship between drawings in a presentation or in a set of construction drawings. This second type of symbol contains text that changes to reflect the location of the referenced drawing or a description of the drawing. While the number of sheets in a presentation or construction drawing will vary from 2 to more than 100, the purpose and use of the drawing symbols is always the same: to create a visual link among the drawings.

For example, a small presentation may contain one floor plan, two building sections, and four interior elevations. The building section symbol is used in the floor plan drawing (sheet A1) to identify the location of the first building section cut and the location of the building section in the presentation (drawing 1 on sheet A2). This symbol will also identify the second building section (drawing 2 on sheet A2). The interior elevation symbol is used on the floor plan to identify the walls that are elevated and the location of the interior elevations in the presentation (drawings 1, 2, 3, and 4 on sheet A3). Examples of these symbols are available in the Chapter 13 folder http://www.fairchildbooks.com/book.cms?bookId=179

This chapter explains what these symbols look like, how to create them, and how to use them in your drawings. Most importantly, you will learn how to create blocks with editable text.

Graphic Drawing Symbols

Presentation drawings and construction drawings may contain several sheets. Drawing symbols are used to coordinate or link the drawings within these sheets. There are a number of standard graphic symbols used in design drawings and construction documents. In AutoCAD, you will create individual blocks with attributed text for each symbol. Text in all drawing symbols is always horizontal to the page.

Drawing Name / Detail Name Symbol

- This symbol is used to identify drawings when more than one drawing exists on a printed sheet. For example, if you have three interior elevations on a sheet, then each elevation would have one of these symbols under it identifying it by name and number.

Exterior Elevation Symbol

- This symbol is used on floor plans to identify exterior elevations. The top number refers to the number in the Drawing Name Symbol on the exterior elevation sheet. The bottom number refers to the exterior elevation sheet number. The arrow in this symbol is rotated to point toward the exterior surface that is elevated.

Building Section Symbol

- This symbol is used on floor plans to identify building sections. The top number refers to the number in the Drawing Name Symbol on the building section sheet. The bottom number refers to the building section sheet number.
- The arrow in this symbol is rotated to point in the direction of the cut.
- The section line typically stops short of the exterior wall on either side of the floor plan.

Grid Symbol

- This symbol is used on floor plans to identify the letter or number of the structural grid. The letters I and O are not used because they look too similar to the numbers 1 and 0.

Interior Elevation Symbol

- This symbol is used on floor plans to identify interior elevations. The perimeter numbers refer to the numbers in the Drawing Name Symbol on the interior elevation sheet. The middle number refers to the interior elevation sheet number.
- This symbol is generally located in the middle of a room with the arrows pointing toward the interior surfaces that are elevated.

DRAWING NAME / DETAIL NAME

EXTERIOR ELEVATION

BUILDING SECTION

GRID

INTERIOR ELEVATION

Guidelines for Creating Symbols

The symbols in this chapter will all be saved as blocks for your use in future projects.

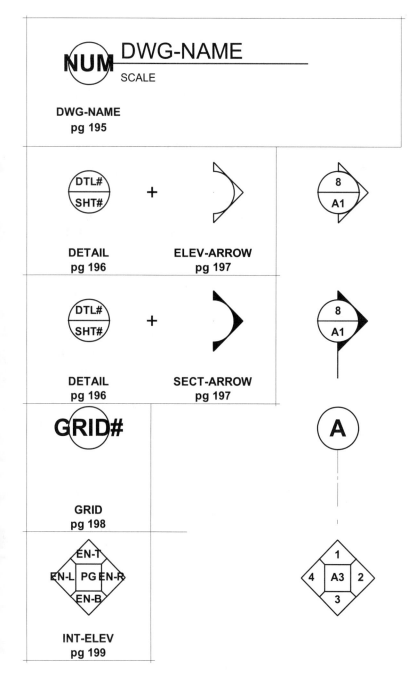

- As shown to the left, some symbols are a combination of multiple blocks.
- Each symbol is listed with its block name and a page number where you can find information about creating the symbol.

The tips below will help you use your symbols in multiple drawings at any scale.

- Know insertion point – the guides on the following pages will identify the desired insertion point. Pay careful attention to these insertion points when creating your blocks.
- Export all your symbols/blocks in a unique symbol directory on your computer.
- Draft your symbols at the size you want them to print. When you insert a symbol into a drawing you can scale it to match the scale of the drawing.

Drawing Symbol Lines

- Draw all the lines in your symbols on layer **0**.
- Use **BYLAYER** color for all lines in your symbol.

Adding Symbol Text

- Unless noted otherwise, create text at **3/32"** tall using the same text style you have chosen for your drawing set.
- Place your text on layer **0**.
- Use **COLOR 4** for all text in your symbol.
- Use Attribute Definition (**ATTDEF**) to create text so you can modify the text in your symbols after you convert them to blocks.

Attributed (Editable) Text

AutoCAD allows you to include informational text within a block and later modify it within your drawing. An attribute definition is the template we will use to create the attributed text.

Attribute Definition ✕

Mode
- ☐ Invisible
- ☐ Constant
- ☐ Verify
- ☐ Preset

Attribute
- Tag: SHT#
- Prompt: Sheet Number
- Value: A1

Insertion Point
- ☒ Specify On Screen
- X:
- Y:
- Z:

Text Options
- Justification: Middle ▽
- Text Style: Standard ▽
- Height: 3/32"
- Rotation: 0

☒ Lock position in block

[OK] [Close] [Help]

Creating Attributed Text

· Type the command **ATTDEF** and press **ENTER**.
· Create a unique name for the **TAG** value. This attribute cannot contain spaces or special characters (e.g., DOOR#).
· The **PROMPT** value is the question AutoCAD will ask you when you edit the attributes for any given block. This value should be descriptive and can contain spaces (e.g., Door Number).
· Make adjustments as required, paying attention to the text **HEIGHT, ROTATION,** and **STYLE**. Text height for most drawing symbols should be **3/32"**.
· The **OK** button will close the Attribute Definition box and allow you to place the attributed text into your drawing.

DTL#
SHT#

Edit Attributes ✕

Block Name: DETAIL

DETAIL NUMBER: 8

SHEET NUMBER: A1

[OK] [Close] [Help]

8
A1

· Attributed text will display its **PROMPT** value until it is added to a block. (Refer to Chapter 9 for creating a block).

· After you create a block with attributed text, you will be prompted to set the initial values for the attributes in that block. Click the **OK** button after you set the value for each variable.

· Your symbol will be placed in the drawing with the values chosen from the previous step.

Inserting Attributed Blocks

The following steps will guide you through the process of adding or inserting an attributed block into your drawing. This process is the same as the process for inserting a regular block, except AutoCAD will prompt you to set each attribute.

Step 1: Type the command **INSERT** and press **ENTER**. This will open the Insert dialog box.

Step 2: The Name drop-down box lists all the blocks that are currently in your drawing. Select the block name from this list.

Step 3: In the Insertion Point section of the dialog box, **CHECK** the **SPECIFY ON-SCREEN** option.

In the Scale section of the dialog box, **UNCHECK** the **SPECIFY ON-SCREEN** option and set the scale values to match the scale factor for your drawing. If your drawing is scaled at 1/8"=1'-0" then set the Scale to **96**.

In the Rotation section of the dialog box, **UNCHECK** the **SPECIFY ON-SCREEN** option and set the angle to **0**.

Step 4: **CLICK** on the **OK** button to insert your block.

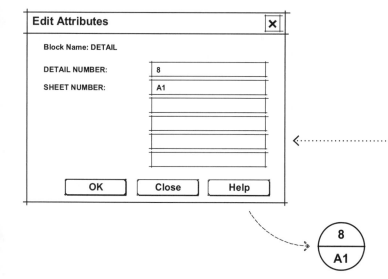

Step 5: After you click the OK button, the Insert dialog box will disappear. The AutoCAD cursor will have the symbol block attached to it.

CLICK ONCE where you want to insert the block. You can modify the position of any block after it is inserted into your drawing.

Step 6: After you position the symbol in your drawing, AutoCAD will prompt you to set the values for this symbol. If you do not see the dialog box, look in the command prompt for further instruction.

Set the values for each variable and **CLICK** on the **OK** button.

Editing Attributed Blocks

You can update attributed text inside an individual block with the Edit Attributes command. This allows you to change the individually set values for each symbol in a single AutoCAD drawing.

- Type the command **ATE** and press **ENTER**.
- **CLICK ONCE** on the block you want to edit.
- When you are finished updating the text attributes, **CLICK** the **OK** button.

- Repeat these steps for each block that you want to update.

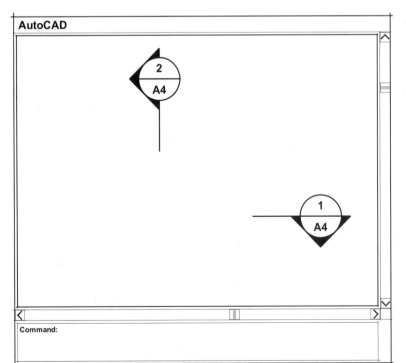

- Even though the two symbols to the left are the same block, you can individually set the text values by using attributed text.

- If the two symbols to the left were created with normal AutoCAD text, you could not set the individual text values.

Creating the Drawing Name Symbol

This symbol is used to identify drawings when more than one drawing exists on a printed sheet. For example, if you have three interior elevations on one sheet, each elevation would have this symbol under it to identify the drawing by name and number.

Drawing the Drawing Name Symbol

· Set the current layer to **0** and the color to **BYLAYER**.
· Draw a circle with a radius of 1/4". Draw a 2-1/2" horizontal line from the right quadrant of the circle.

Add Attributed Text to the Drawing Symbol

You need to add three attributed text definitions to your block. The first is for the drawing number, the second is for the drawing name, and the third is for the scale of the drawing.

· Set the current layer to **0** and the color to **BLUE (5)**.
· Type the command **ATTDEF** and press **ENTER**. This will open the Attribute Definition dialog box.

· Set the Attribute Tag to: **NUM**
· Set the Attribute Prompt to: **DRAWING NUMBER**
· Set the remaining attributes to match the drawing to the left.
· **CLICK** the **OK** button and place the text in the middle of the circle.
· Follow the steps above to create the second and third attributed text definitions. Place each as indicated in the drawing above.

Creating a Block of the Symbol

· Create a block of the symbol using the **BLOCK** command.
· Set the Base Point for the block at the center of the circle.
· Name the block **DWG-NAME**.

· Export the block to a symbols folder on your computer using the **WBLOCK** command.

Creating the Detail Symbol

The detail symbol is used in combination with the exterior elevation or section arrow (facing page) on floor plans to identify exterior elevations and building sections. The bottom number in this symbol references the sheet number where the exterior elevation or building section is drawn. The top number in this symbol matches the Drawing Name Symbol on the exterior elevation or building section sheet.

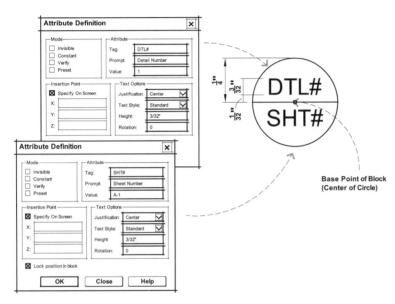

Drawing the Detail Symbol

· Set the current layer to **0** and the color to **BYLAYER**.
· Draw a circle with a radius of 1/4". Draw a horizontal line through the middle of the circle.

Add Attributed Text to the Detail Symbol

You need to add two attributed text definitions to your block. The first is for the detail number, the second is for the sheet number.

· Set the current layer to **0** and the color to **BLUE (5)**.
· Type the command **ATTDEF** and press **ENTER**. This will open the Attribute Definition dialog box.
· Set the Attribute Tag to: **DTL#**.
· Set the Attribute Prompt to: **DETAIL NUMBER**.
· Set the remaining attributes to match the drawing to the left.
· **CLICK** the **OK** button and place the text in the middle of the circle above the horizontal line.

· Follow the steps above to create a second attributed text definition for the sheet number.
· Set the Attribute Tag to: **SHT#**.
· Set the Attribute Prompt to: **SHEET NUMBER**.
· Set the remaining attributes to match the drawing to the left.
· **CLICK** the **OK** button and place the text in the middle of the circle below the horizontal line.

Creating a Block of the Symbol

· Create a block of the symbol using the **BLOCK** command.
· Set the Base Point for the block at the center of the circle.
· Name the block **DETAIL**.

· Export the block to a symbols folder on your computer using the **WBLOCK** command.

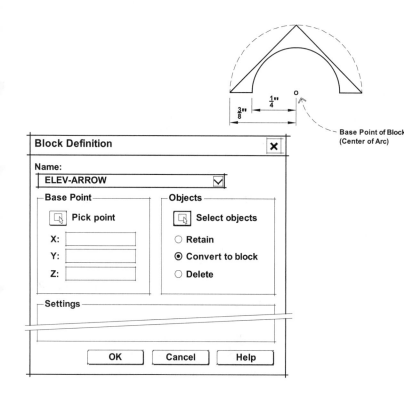

Base Point of Block
(Center of Arc)

Creating the Section and Exterior Elevation Arrows

These symbols are used in combination with the detail symbol (facing page) on floor plans to identify exterior elevations and building sections. The arrow in this symbol is rotated to point toward the exterior surface that is elevated or in the direction of the section cut.

Drawing the Exterior Elevation Arrow

· Set the current layer to **0** and the color to **BYLAYER**.
· Draw a circle with a radius of 1/4". Trim the lower half of the circle. Complete the arrow using the **QUADRANT** snaps of a second circle 3/8" in diameter.

Creating a Block of the Symbol

· Create a block of the symbol using the **BLOCK** command.
· Set the Base Point for the block at the center of the circle.
· Name the block **ELEV-ARROW**.

· Export the block to a symbols folder on your computer using the **WBLOCK** command.

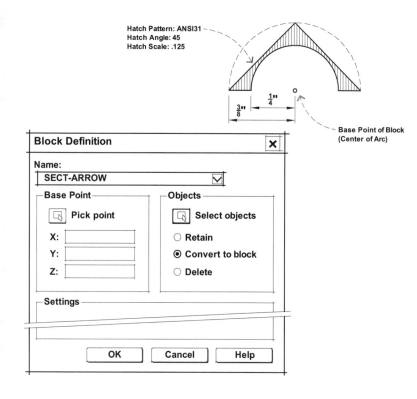

Hatch Pattern: ANSI31
Hatch Angle: 45
Hatch Scale: .125

Base Point of Block
(Center of Arc)

Drawing the Section Arrow

· Set the current layer to **0** and the color to **BYLAYER**.
· Draw a circle with a radius of 1/4". Trim the lower half of the circle. Complete the arrow using the **QUADRANT** snaps of a second circle 3/8" in diameter.
· Fill the arrow with the hatch pattern ANSI31.

Creating a Block of the Symbol

· Create a block of the symbol using the **BLOCK** command.
· Set the Base Point for the block at the center of the circle.
· Name the block **SECT-ARROW**.

· Export the block to a symbols folder on your computer using the **WBLOCK** command.

Creating the Grid Symbol

This symbol is used on floor plans to identify the letter or number of the structural grid. The letters I and O are not used because they look too similar to the numbers 1 and 0. The text in this symbol is always horizontal to the page.

Drawing the Grid Symbol

· Set the current layer to **0** and the color to **BYLAYER**.
· Draw a circle with a radius of 1/4".

Add Attributed Text to the Grid Symbol

You need to add one attributed text definition to your block.

· Set the current layer to **0** and the color to **BLUE (5)**.
· Type the command **ATTDEF** and press **ENTER**. This will open the Attribute Definition dialog box.
· Set the Attribute Tag to: **GRID#**
· Set the Attribute Prompt to: **GRID NUMBER**
· Set the remaining attributes to match the drawing to the left.
· **CLICK** the **OK** button and place the text in the middle of the circle above the horizontal line.

Creating a Block of the Symbol

· Create a block of the symbol using the **BLOCK** command.
· Set the Base Point for the block at the center of the circle.
· Name the block **GRID**.

· Export the block to a symbols folder on your computer using the **WBLOCK** command.

Creating the Interior Elevation Symbol

This symbol is used on floor plans to identify interior elevations. The numbers match the Drawing Name Symbol number on the interior elevation sheet. This symbol is generally located in the middle of a room with the arrows pointing toward the interior surfaces that are elevated.

Drawing the Interior Elevation Symbol

· Set the current layer to **0** and the color to **BYLAYER**.
· Draw a square with sides measuring **5/16"**. Draw a second square with sides measuring **5/8"**. Center the larger square on the smaller square and rotate it 45 degrees. Complete the symbol to match the one drawn to the left.

Add Attributed Text to the Grid Symbol

You need to add five attributed text definitions to your block.

· Set the current layer to **0** and the color to **BLUE (5)**.
· Type the command **ATTDEF** and press **ENTER**. This will open the Attribute Definition dialog box.
· Set the Attribute Tag to: **SHT**
· Set the Attribute Prompt to: **SHEET NUMBER**
· Set the remaining attributes to match the drawing to the left.
· **CLICK** the **OK** button and place the text in the middle of the small circle.

· Create four more attributed text definitions for each of the elevations (top, right, left, and bottom).

Creating a Block of the Symbol

· Create a block of the symbol using the **BLOCK** command.
· Set the Base Point for the block at the center of the small square.
· Name the block **INT-ELEV**.

· Export the block to a symbols folder on your computer using the **WBLOCK** command.

1 EAMES HOUSE - FIRST FLOOR PLAN
SCALE: 1/8"=1'-0"

Learning Exercise

In this exercise, you will add grid symbols and a drawing title to your floor plan.

Open Your Drawing

· Open AutoCAD.
· Open the drawing you created in the previous chapter:
  DDFD-EAMES.DWG

Creating Your Layers

Create the following layers:

· **A-SYMBOL**   Color 4
· Set the current layer to **A-SYMBOL**.

Adding the Grid Symbols

· Using the **INSERT** command, add the grid number symbol you created earlier in this chapter to your drawing as indicated above.
· Use the **ATE** command to adjust the value of each symbol.
· Notice that the symbol is used only on grids that intersect a column.

· Save your drawing.

Adding the Drawing Symbol

· Using the **INSERT** command, add the drawing symbol you created earlier in this chapter to your drawing as indicated above.
· The horizontal line in the symbol is most likely not long enough to extend past the name of your drawing. You can draw an extension line either to the end of the drawing name or to the end of the drawing (shown above).

· Save your drawing.

Congratulations, you have completed the learning exercise for this chapter.

CHAPTER 14

Linking Drawings/ External References

In Chapter 9, you learned how to use blocks to import symbols into an AutoCAD drawing. External References (Xrefs) are conceptually very close to blocks. Just like blocks, Xrefs allow you to import drawings like a title block into any other AutoCAD drawing with one advantage: External references will automatically import changes made to the original drawing.

In larger design firms, Xrefs are primarily used to link title sheets and floor plans. They allow you to quickly and easily update an entire set of drawings.

- If you need to change the issue date for a presentation or a set of construction drawings, you can update the references title sheet and every drawing in the set will automatically update.

- If you change the location of a door in a room or office in the referenced floor plan, then every plan (enlarged, reflected ceiling plan, finish plan, furniture plan, and so on) in the drawing set will automatically update.

Drawing with Overlays

When you draw by hand, you may overlay several sheets of drafting mylar to see the relationship between drawings. This technique is commonly used in reflected ceiling plans so the designer does not have to redraw the floor plan. Overlay both sheets, run it through the blueprint machine, and you have a combined drawing.

Floor Plan

This drawing usually contains all of the floor plan information that may find its way into the final floor plan, the reflected ceiling plan, and other enlarged floor plans.

· When you update the base plan (e.g., move a wall or a door), all other overlaid drawings are updated.

Title Sheet

This drawing contains the page border and generic project information. It can be overlaid onto every drawing in your presentation or drawing set.

· When you make a change to the title sheet (e.g., change the submission date or project phone number), all other overlaid drawings are updated.

Drawing with XREFS

When you draw in AutoCAD, you can link several drawings to see the relationship between drawings. This technique is commonly used to link title sheets to floor plans, reflected ceiling plans, and elevations. XREFS help the designer quickly update title sheet items (like a presentation date) for every drawing.

Base Floor Plan

This drawing usually contains all of the floor plan information that may find its way into the final floor plan, the reflected ceiling plan, and other enlarged floor plans.

- In AutoCAD, you can link this base floor plan to Model Space of multiple plans or formatted sheets.
- When you update the base plan (e.g., move a wall or a door), all other drawings that link to the base floor plan are automatically updated.
- You can adjust the layer color and layer visibility in linked drawings.

Title Sheet

This drawing contains the page border and generic project information. It will be linked to every drawing in your presentation or drawing set.

- In AutoCAD, you can link the title sheet to the layout view of every formatted sheet.
- When you update the title sheet (e.g., change the submission date or project phone number), all other drawings that link to the title sheet are automatically updated.

XREF Manager

The XREF Manager displays Xrefs in your current drawing. It also allows you to add new XREFS to your drawing or modify Xrefs currently attached to your drawings.

AutoCAD 2007

AutoCAD 2006 and earlier

Opening the XREF Manager

· Type the command **XREF** and press **ENTER**.

2007 XREF Manager

· The **ATTACH** button allows you to add an Xrefs to your drawing.

· The **REFRESH** button will refresh an Xref in your current drawing. This can be helpful if you have made changes in a referenced drawing but do not see the changes reflected in the current drawing.

2006 and Earlier XREF Manager

The **TREE VIEW** and **LIST VIEW** buttons adjust the display methods for the Xref Manager.

· The **LIST VIEW** is the default view. It shows a list of all Xrefs in the current drawing.
· The **TREE VIEW** shows the relationship between all Xrefs and the current drawing.

· The **ATTACH** button allows you to add an Xref to your drawing.

· The **DETACH** button allows you to remove one or more Xrefs from your drawing.

· The **RELOAD** button will refresh an Xref in your current drawing. This can be helpful if you have made changes in a referenced drawing but do not see the changes reflected in the current drawing.

· The **UNLOAD** button will visibly remove an Xref from your drawing. The drawing can be turned back on at any time by clicking the reload button.

· The **BIND** button allows you to insert one or more Xrefs into the current drawing. This will break the link between the referenced drawing and the current drawing.

Adding an XREF to Your Drawing

To complete the following exercise you will need a title sheet drawing and a plan or elevation drawing.

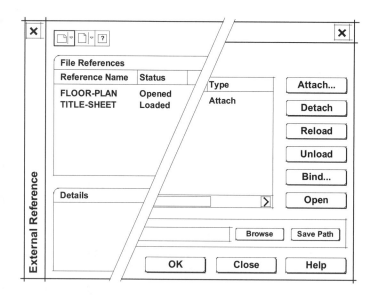

- **Step 1:** Open the plan or elevation drawing in AutoCAD and switch to a layout view (Paper Space). Set the current layer to **0**.
- **Step 2:** Type the command **XREF** and press **ENTER**.
- **Step 3:** **CLICK ONCE** on the **ATTACH** button. This will open a File dialog box. Locate your title block file on your computer and click the **OPEN** button.

- **Step 4:** Set the Reference Type to: **ATTACHMENT**
- **Step 5:** Set the Path Type to: **FULL PATH**
- **Step 6:** Set the X, Y, and Z coordinates of Insertion Point to: **0**
- **Step 7:** **CLICK ONCE** on the **OK** button.

- The title sheet will be attached to the layout view of your elevation or plan drawing.
- Modify the size or scale of the viewport in this layout.
- Adjust the page layout for this view to match your title sheet.

- Save your drawing.

XREF Strategies for Individual Designers

If you have one or two designers working on a project, you can use the following XREF strategy to set up your plans. This strategy minimizes the number of drawings required to complete a drawing set. (Two AutoCAD drawings are created to plot four different floor plans.)

Title Sheet

- Create a title sheet that contains your page border and generic project information.
- Draw all information in Model Space of the title sheet AutoCAD drawing.
- Name the drawing **TITLE-SHEET.DWG**

Floor Plan Drawing

- Create a second drawing that contains your floor plan information.
- Use a layer strategy that allows you to print different types of plans from the same drawing.
- Name the drawing **PLAN-1.DWG**

Floor Plan Layouts (Tabs)

- Create a unique layout for each plan type.
- XREF **TITLE-SHEET.DWG** into each layout (Paper Space).
- Freeze layers (current viewport freeze) for each layout. This will allow you to print the demo plan from the Demo Layout tab without the furniture layer turned on.

XREF Strategies for Multiple Designers

If you have multiple designers working on a project, you can use the following XREF strategy to set up your plans. This strategy maximizes the number of drawings that can be edited by different designers. (Six AutoCAD drawings are created to plot four different floor plans.)

Title Sheet

- Create a title sheet that contains your page border and generic project information.
- Draw all information in Model Space of the title sheet AutoCAD drawing.
- Name the drawing **TITLE-SHEET.DWG**

Base Floor Plan Drawing

- Create a second drawing that contains your base floor plan information.
- Minimize sheet-specific text and dimensions. This information will be placed in the formatted sheet drawings.
- Name the drawing **XPLAN-1.DWG**

Formatted Sheets

- Create a unique drawing for each plan type.
- XREF **XPLAN-1.DWG** into Model Space.
- XREF **TITLE-SHEET.DWG** into Paper Space.
- Add additional information in Model Space such as room names, dimensions, notes, and door tags.
- Name the drawing similar to its sheet number. Therefore, sheet A1.1 would be named **A1-1.DWG**.

Elevation XREF Strategies for Individual Designers

If you have one or two designers working on a project, you can use the following XREF strategy to set up your elevation. This strategy minimizes the number of drawings required to complete a drawing set. (Two AutoCAD drawings are created to plot four different elevation sheets.)

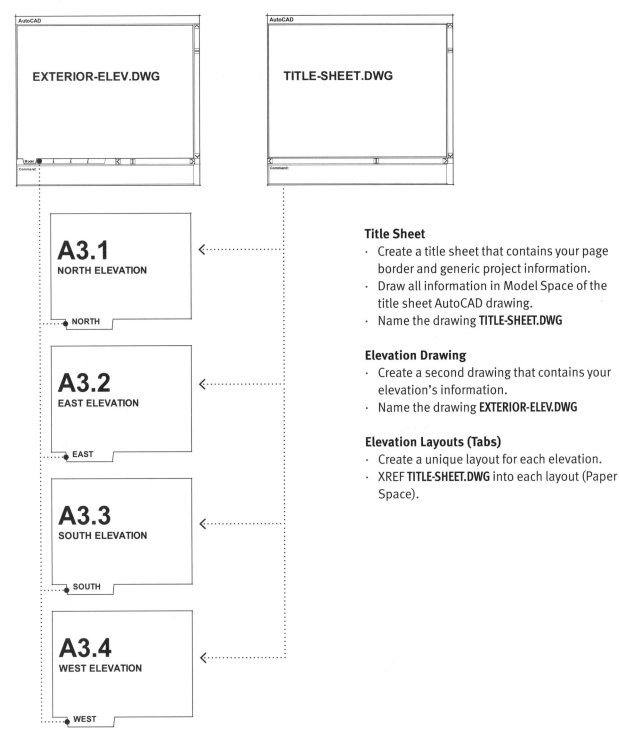

Title Sheet

· Create a title sheet that contains your page border and generic project information.
· Draw all information in Model Space of the title sheet AutoCAD drawing.
· Name the drawing **TITLE-SHEET.DWG**

Elevation Drawing

· Create a second drawing that contains your elevation's information.
· Name the drawing **EXTERIOR-ELEV.DWG**

Elevation Layouts (Tabs)

· Create a unique layout for each elevation.
· XREF **TITLE-SHEET.DWG** into each layout (Paper Space).

Elevation XREF Strategies for Multiple Designers

If you have multiple designers working on a project, you can use the following XREF strategy to set up your elevations. This strategy maximizes the number of drawings that can be edited by different designers. (Six AutoCAD drawings are created to plot four different elevations).

Title Sheet

- Create a title sheet that contains your page border and generic project information.
- Draw all information in Model Space of the title sheet AutoCAD drawing.
- Name the drawing **TITLE-SHEET.DWG**

Base Elevation Drawing

- Create a second drawing that contains your base elevation information.
- Minimize sheet-specific text and dimensions. This information will be placed in the formatted sheet drawings.
- Name the drawing **XELEV.DWG**

Formatted Sheets

- Create a unique drawing for each plan type.
- XREF **XELEV.DWG** into Model Space.
- XREF **TITLE-SHEET.DWG** into Paper Space.
- Add additional information in Model Space such as room names, dimensions, notes, and door tags.
- Name the drawing similar to its sheet number. Therefore, sheet A3.1 would be named **A3-1.DWG**.

① **EAMES HOUSE - FIRST FLOOR PLAN**
  SCALE: 1/8"=1'-0"

Learning Exercise

In this exercise, you will complete your floor plan by adding the casework and a graphic scale.

Open Your Drawing

· Open AutoCAD.
· Open the drawing you created in the previous chapter:
  DDFD-EAMES.DWG

Creating Your Layers

Create the following layers:

· **A-CASE**   Color 5
· Set the current layer to **A-CASE.**

Adding the Casework

· Cabinets are drawn on their own layer and are typically 24" deep. Add the cabinets to your drawing to match those in the drawing above. The cabinets are indicated by a light gray poché.

· Save your drawing.

Adding a Graphic Symbol

· Set the current layer to **A-SYMBOL.**

· Draw the graphic scale to match the one above. Typically, graphic scales are coordinated with the scale of the drawing. Because this drawing is 1/8"=1'-0", the graphic symbol will mark the 1", 4", and 8" distances. If this drawing was 1/16"=1'-0", the graphic symbol would mark the 1", 8", and 16" distances.

· Save your drawing.

Congratulations, you have completed the learning exercise for this chapter.

CONCLUSION

AutoCAD continues to dominate the two-dimensional drafting market-place for architects and interior designers. Fifteen years ago, it was not possible to work in a design office or academic environment without a prerequisite knowledge of hand drafting. Today, universities and employers demand a strong understanding of digital drawing with AutoCAD. Through the completion of this book, your new technical skills and conceptual understanding of digital drawing with AutoCAD will help you excel in both the design studio and the office. This foundation will also help you quickly adapt to future releases of AutoCAD.

Because each page in this book is designed to maximize learning, you can quickly access and practice specific AutoCAD concepts and commands necessary during busy workweeks or studio deadlines. That said, it is important to reflect on the knowledge and understanding gained through each section of this book.

Hand Drawing and Digital Drawing: In Chapter 1 through Chapter 4, you were introduced to AutoCAD and digital drawing through the language and concepts of manual or hand drawing. Lines, circles, and arcs are the fundamental building blocks of all architectural drawings. Your expanded understanding of the various methods to create and modify these building blocks in AutoCAD allows you to create any type of drawing.

Design Drawings: Chapter 5 through Chapter 8 introduced you to graphic standards that help you use AutoCAD to communicate your design ideas. Understanding these standards keeps you in control of your drawing and allows you to "ask of the computer" rather than let the computer dictate how your drawings will look. In these chapters, you also increased your understanding of drawing and organizational strategies in AutoCAD.

Advanced Drawing Tools: In the final chapters of this book, you were introduced to many advanced AutoCAD concepts, such as dimensioning drawings, creating your own drawing stencils, and linking drawings. By combining these advanced concepts with your strong foundation for drawing in AutoCAD, you will be prepared to work on or create any digital drawing.

Today, a strong understanding of digital drawing with AutoCAD is required of almost every professional designer. Your insight into how to use AutoCAD to communicate design ideas will help place you at the top of most hire lists. It is my hope that the visual guides and pedagogical approach of this book have helped you become a stronger designer.

INDEX

QUICK REFERENCE GUIDE

Drawing Commands
Line   12, 13, 14, 15
RECtangle   17
Dashed lines   118

Ortho (**F8**)   4, 14
Units   5, 22
Running Object Snaps (**F3**)   21

Circle   16
Arc   18

LAyer Properties Manager   56

Viewport (**VP**)   96–98

Text   103–109

Hatch (**BH**)   113–117

insert Block   131
Polyline (**PL**)   38–39

Viewing and navigating your drawing
Pan (mouse scroll wheel)   8
Zoom (mouse scroll wheel)   9
Zoom Extents (**Z ENTER, E ENTER**)   9

Cleaning your drawing
Purge   141
Audit   141

Editing your drawing
Erase   13
Undo   23

COpy   29
Move   28
MIrror   31
ROtate   30

TRim   40
EXtend   41
Fillet   43
Offset   42

BReak   46
EXplode   46

MAtch properties   139
CHange properties   138

SCale   140
Stretch   32

Dimensioning your drawing
DIstance   139

Dimensions   150–170
Text leaders   178